Creating Creativity
Innovation Techniques for Business, Managers and Entrepreneurs

by Thomas Van Hare

Edited by Helena Nolke

Also by Thomas Van Hare, with co-author Matt Lawrence:

BETRAYAL: Clinton, Castro & the Cuban Five
TRAICIÓN: Clinton, Castro y Los Cinco Cubanos (Spanish Edition)

Also by Thomas Van Hare with co-author Helena Nolke:

Famously Michigan: a Quotable Journey through the State

Cover design and book artwork by Thomas Van Hare
www.digitalminute.com

Printed and Kindle Edition: July 2015

To my family

No cows were harmed in the writing of this book.

ᛏᛁᛄᚻᚱᛁᛗᚾ

Table of Contents

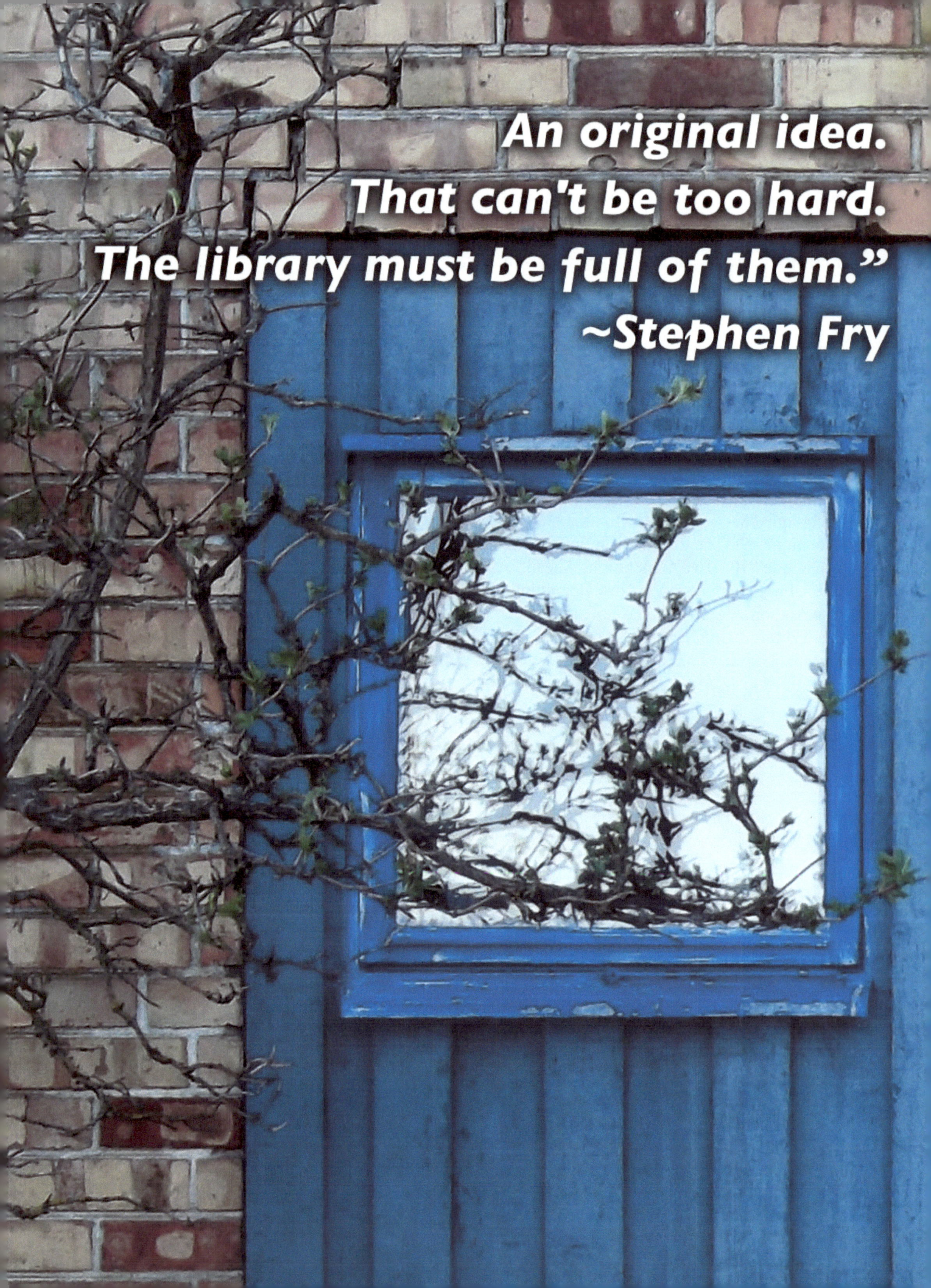

An original idea.
That can't be too hard.
The library must be full of them."
~Stephen Fry

Introduction – A Creatively-Challenged World

Most managers typically view themselves as innovative, highly creative thinkers. Yet many would cite a lack of creativity in their businesses as being one of their key challenges. If pressed and asked to detail the new ideas of their own, very few can cite even one or two transformational events that they authored in their workplace. Surprisingly, this holds true as much for established, "old style" businesses as it does for new, entrepreneurial ones. Even the much vaunted technology sector suffers from a lack of creativity. Despite its extraordinary potential, creativity remains the orphan stepchild of business. The good news is that virtually everyone has a vast well of untapped creativity hidden within themselves. When the full staff and business team are properly organized and directed in a way that encourages creative thinking, the potential for change is enormous – and profits are bound to increase, as enthusiasm, job satisfaction and well-being. Stresses are reduced, employee turnover is decreased and the business becomes a magnet for the best and brightest.

The goal of this book is to provide you with a set of tools and techniques that will enable you to encourage, foster and harness creativity in yourself and in your business. _Creating Creativity_ provides you with the hows, ifs, whys and whats of creativity. It teaches you how to hold a creative session and how to change your management style so that you can focus on creativity every day – whether you are working with the entire office, in small groups or alone. By applying the techniques outlined in this book, you can transform your business, improve your management technique and expand your potential. You will no longer view work as "work", but rather you will see it as a creative challenge and an opportunity _"to do the vision thing."_ Even the most boring job can be the springboard for innovation – in fact, it is often at the most boring jobs that the potential of creativity is at its greatest.

The lessons of this book apply equally to manufacturers, distribution businesses, logistics companies, service industries, the military, non-profit groups, and even to government and public service. Regarding the latter, for many, the idea of a government employee practicing creativity might seem like an oxymoron. That view is dead wrong. Indeed, some of the most effective, brilliant and capable managers I've ever encountered have been in the halls of government, at the White House, in the Pentagon, and on Capitol Hill.

In fact, for government employees, this book has particular relevance. With a proliferation of laws, limits, restrictions and policies, the dull landscape of daily work is naturally more challenging than it is in private business. Once you finish this book, you will realize why that also means that the opportunity for using creativity is there at its greatest too.

A Note about the Creative Techniques in this Book

The creative techniques in this book are all proven models that have withstood the test of time. Each has been used in countless creative sessions. Most of these techniques were developed and tested in my former advertising and design studio. Some are original and some have been learned from others over the years. As the heads of various agencies and design studios get together, a popular topic is comparing process and creative techniques with others. Some of these techniques were learned with experience in the halls of government. Others were learned while working overseas in defense and security matters. Advertising and design, however, is the ultimate proving ground for creative technique since the very foundation of the work product is the Idea. To be successful in advertising and design, you begin and end with the Idea. Everything else is window dressing, even if most clients rarely see past the lintels and door frames of the house of ideas that you build and present. Pretty pictures may sell clients but ideas drive sales and profits.

Based on these experiences, encompassing a working career of nearly four decades years, I have periodically been asked to lecture on the processes and techniques of creative thinking. My one conclusion is that idea generation is hard – and it is also easy. I have addressed numerous forums and international conferences, including the HOW Design Conference, which I was honored to both attend and be asked to lecture on design three times over the years. At my last HOW Design Conference, no fewer than 350 designers and advertising professionals attended my speech, proving that even professional creatives are hungry for creative guidance, new techniques and methods.

In addition, I have been engaged by numerous companies to assist them in understanding how to apply creative processes to their unique business challenges both within the USA and aboard. Often, I am called to assist in product development and in advising on innovation, invention and new ideas.

My expertise ranges from government and security, to international relations, the aviation sector, advertising and graphic design. Lest you think of me as some creative super hero, rest assured that I am dreadfully unorganized at home and, as my wife will take pleasure in pointing out, deeply flawed too. My desk is regularly little more than a mess of piled papers. Despite this, I am highly organized and focused at work – that too is one of the hallmarks of creative people. I split my time between work at home in the USA on the East Coast and aboard in Scandinavia, where I find that numerous businesses are very open to the idea of creative sessions, creative thinking and creativity-focused management.

In recent years, I've taken to not only helping others with their businesses but launching my own. Put simply, I took what I know of creativity and held my own sessions – the result is the creation of a new commercial lighting system, the filing of a patent and the launch of a new business that I expect will finally make me the profits that I have made for so many others over the years when working as a hired consultant. My new business is called American Skystar Lighting. You can find it online at: *www.AmericanSkystar.com*.

My consulting company, *Digital Minute,* is online at: *www.digitalminute.com*. If you would like assistance or have any questions, please email me at: *tvanhare@digitalminute.com*.

I look forward to hearing from you.

– Thomas Van Hare

cre·a·tiv·i·ty
/ˌkrēāˈtivitē/

1. the state of being creative.

2. to transcend or go beyond traditional ideas; to introduce new rules and relationships.

3. to originate new products, services, forms, interpretations, techniques and methods.

4. the process of thinking whereby one engages creative ability or knowledge.

5. to transform a process through innovation.

Origin: From late 14th C., orig. derived from Latin, *creatus*, pp. of *creare* "to produce, grow, make."

Sometimes imagination pounces; mostly it sleeps soundly in the corner, purring.
~Terri Guillemets

Chapter 1 – Building Creativity into Your Business

We live in a world of creativity – every product and service around us was created and designed by someone. We are surrounded by original thoughts that, over time, have become the accepted practices, things and basic requirements of our lives. Indeed, we have literally designed the world to our own liking and, never satisfied, we continue to design it and redesign anew it every day. Most often we fail to honor those inventors who came before and made our life what it is today. We simply take their creativity and innovations for granted. Look around – you will quickly recognize that we are surrounded by revolutionary ideas and things, everything from the paint on the walls, to the chair you sit on, to the clothes you wear and even the letters and words you read now. In other words, somebody made that door knob and your life is changed as a result. The revolution of new ideas is ongoing and never ending.

Future generations will look upon our present world through the lens of their own countless innovations, ideas and changes. They will consider us almost as a primitive species, as if we are an alien life form, or worse yet, as vestiges of mankind's history, a sorry, sordid tale of mistakes, triumphs, joys and disasters. They will wonder how we could have lived with so many challenges. Even today, we wonder how the last generation lived without WiFi. A generation from now, the WiFi connected world will be studied as an interesting historic technology and nothing more. Just as people of the past lived without WiFi, so too will people of the future, but for different reasons.

Our world is daily transformed by our creative efforts – for good or for bad. Mother Nature only peeks around the corner in varying degrees, perhaps casting a disapproving glance at us from underneath the asphalt of our parking lots or from between the shrubs and bushes of our carefully manicured lawns and gardens. She sits shyly by, installed in potted plants on window sills which we think that by watering, careful pruning, we create into something of art and beauty. Though I digress, it cannot be denied that our daily life is creatively wrought in plastics, woven with fabrics, hammered into shapes in metals, forged into devices, molded together into useful instruments and burned for fuel. We have tamed our world upside down and hammered it into our own vision.

Yes, for good and for bad.

This spark of creativity drives the cycles of history. You see creativity at work when the first cavemen worked out how to light a fire and warm the cave. Later, another spark of imagination lead someone to cook food. That was over a million years ago. The first dinner in the cave probably had some kid complaining that someone had to invent ketchup or they wouldn't eat their vegetables.

You can catch a glimpse of creativity on the march when ancient Persians herded the first group of aurochs together and began breeding them down to become the modern cow. You can even find evidence of it in the most recent times when digital inventors publish apps that run on your smart phone. Each generation is ushered forward with an unending, accelerating stream of invention. We begin and end each cycle of history with new ideas, whether big or small. Above all, what matters most is innovation – everything else, from basic survival to profit in business, is simply the natural result of innovation.

Know this well – we are surrounded by creativity. We are all inventors at heart, born with creativity. We live lives of unending cycles of creative thought. The power of ideas is so great that, if I didn't know better, I would suspect that mankind even invented God. Can you imagine that somehow we can imagine the infinite?

Despite the obvious business benefits that come from creativity, many entrepreneurs and managers have extraordinary difficulty harnessing and encouraging it in the workplace. Creativity brings change and revolution. Yet it is not all welcome and rosy, good news stories. These are the very things that are most feared in a world. Most people are strangely conflicted between seeking change and the balancing force of the desire to enjoy the stability of the status quo. Carefully wrought plans, perfectly calculated budgets, adjusted accounting balance sheets and highly evolved organizations are the enemies of free thought, but also its necessary enabling force. Without these things, ideas would never be put into action. You cannot have light without darkness and vice-versa.

True creativity is hard. It takes work. The "Eureka Moment" does not happen everyday – it is born of effort and concentration. Archimedes did not invent his wheel with a singular, effortless "Eureka!" His inventions were the product of a lifetime of hard work, thinking, learning, reasoning and creating. A famous story in art concerns a painting by Whistler. When sold, it commanded a high price. Upon discovering that the painting had taken less than a day to create, the buyer filed a lawsuit claiming that the rate charged, if computed per hour, was abusively high. Whistler's attorneys responded with the simple argument that the painting itself was not created in just a day, rather it was the product of a lifetime of study and work by the artist. That experience had culminated into a single day's worth of creativity with a brush and paint upon paper. They argued that the final day of painting could not have been accomplished without the experience gained in the years before.

Some modern, digital companies have made extraordinary efforts to authorize and encourage creativity – two such examples are Google and Apple. In the case of Google, employees are given time each week to work on their own creative ideas. Many of the most impressive innovations in Google's tableau of products and services have their roots in these employee projects. Likewise, at Apple, employees are granted access to leadership based not on rank within the workplace hierarchy, but on the power of their ideas and innovations. Apple is a company that until 2011 was run day-to-day by the late Steve Jobs, a man whose self-selected main role was as "chief creative," not as CEO.

Nonetheless, most cutting edge (or bleeding edge) entrepreneurs only practice creativity in very limited ways. It is the norm that creativity ends once the *Big Idea* is born and the new business, product or service is launched. Sadly, for most businesses, creativity is stifled two feet beyond the door to the head office.

When I see a Suggestion Box hung on the wall, I know I have entered the halls of a creatively-challenged business.

It is not just management elitism, fear of change or the difficulties involved in developing new ideas that keeps creativity on the back burner. There are many other reasons as well, including:

- Most businesses, even new start-ups, cite a lack of time to be creative, which is viewed as a luxury in the press of day-to-day events and tasks.

- The force of institutional practice channels employees to not challenge the way things are done, which, particularly on established businesses, is wrongly dictated by obscure company policy and working tradition.

- The very terms of business language inadvertently discourage creativity and encourage criticism; this forms a "built-in" judgmental response system that tends to smother ideas and kill creative thought.

- There are few rewards in the short- and mid-term for creativity, leaving most employees with few incentives to exercise creative initiative.

- Management rarely takes the time to promote creativity and rarely encourages employees to offer creative inputs because there are often no *direct* and *immediate* benefits seen.

- Employee inputs are usually interpreted as unwelcome challenges to management and to established policy.

- Creativity is not fostered in ways that invite creative input from employees, such as through a forum that is free of judgment and free of ridicule.

- Creativity is loud; it is not easily silenced. It is revolutionary and daring. It is risky. To the extent that we all fear risk, creativity is seen as the enemy. It takes courage, above all, to dare to dream and create.

- Finally, as already mentioned, creativity is hard work. It takes the supreme effort of mind and body to truly be innovative. We all suffer from laziness; it is usually easier to just get along and continue to live our lives safely, unremarkably and quietly.

Despite the central importance of creativity in business, the topic of creative idea formation is poorly covered in literature. We are bombarded with books about accounting methods, writing business plans, managing budgets and improving efficiency. We have dozens or perhaps even hundreds of management technique books. Somehow, creativity is the one area that receives the least attention among authors and publishers, even if it can yield the greatest impact on profitability and business success. The reasons for this are complex and many. Ultimately, it comes down to the point that writing about the subject is hard – indeed, it is as hard as practicing creativity is in the first place.

In this book I present ten techniques for you to use that develop, foster and engage creativity within your business. I have taken the risk to propose a system of creativity and a philosophy that is centered on a single goal – to unleash the power of ideas, not just to improve your business, but also to improve the lot of us all. I lay out a roadmap to transform the challenges of creative-focused thinking into fun and interesting exercises. I provide methods to shift the focus from seeking one *Big Idea* to instead generating hundreds of smaller ideas every week. Taken together, these ideas have the power to transform a business from the bottom up. Along the way, the ideas I present offer the means to build employee morale, increase loyalty, reduce costs, enhance revenues and create better products, services and systems. Above all, who can know when a small idea, one of hundreds, suddenly becomes the *Big Idea* that will take over the world – okay, maybe not take over the world, but you get the idea....

The techniques I present in this book are taken from my experiences running an advertising and design agency and from my years working in marketing, international security and politics. Some techniques were learned during my years in government. Others were developed in my design studio as ways to generate higher power ideas from a staff of creative artists and designers. These techniques have been proven in the marketplace. All have been tested dozens and sometimes hundreds of times, and have shown their value in the real world while addressing real business problems.

This book is designed to help business managers solve their most difficult business challenges, to identify new processes, to enter new markets and to launch new products and services. As well, this book is designed not just for senior business leaders, but also for midlevel and even junior managers new to the workplace – and even for employees at the very bottom. This book is for anyone who seeks to encourage and engage creativity and the power of ideas in the workplace.

My book is equally useful for entrepreneurs and start-ups as it is for established businesses. It is a powerful tool for new product design and for conceptualizing new service offerings. It works on either side of the accounting equation – whether for containing costs or for increasing revenues. This book applies also to processes, staffing, organization and policy development. It can help commercial businesses, non-profit businesses, government entities, arts organizations and even military operations.

> *Creativity and innovation are a basic human trait – yet surprisingly, they are not a basic business trait. Therefore, in business, your key challenge is to stop fighting against nature and instead to create creativity every day.*

Finally, this book offers a guide to tapping into the creativity you have within yourself and to drawing creativity out of your staff and team. It gives you innovative techniques to apply to the challenges of your business – starting today.

Remember always that the lessons of creativity are universal. Likewise, the power of ideas is infinite.

"To unpathed waters,
undreamed shores."
~Shakespeare

Chapter 2 – The When, Where and How of Creativity

To be successful in business, creativity should be invited everywhere, from everyone, all the time. There is no area of business great or small that does not benefit from creativity, even when the challenges are the most severe. Creativity is best applied to problems that are *not easily solved* – and this is where the benefits of creative energy are greatest. Even when the very survival of a company is at risk, and perhaps above all even then, it is time for creativity and decisiveness. To achieve results, creativity must be consciously identified as the key to business success, whether in good times or bad.

To begin, I ask you to consider that virtually every business has untapped creativity that can be found among its staff and managers. Yet without a formal outlet, creativity usually lies quietly dormant. Without direct encouragement to enable creative thinking, the staff will never reach its highest potential.

> *A key challenge for managers in the "new economy" is to encourage and channel creativity for the benefit of the business, its shareholders, management, employees and customers.*

Over the last two decades, the mission of companies and management has changed. The globalized, new digital economy has transformed the workplace, trade, markets finance and economics. Products, services and manufacturing techniques are no longer the crowning capabilities of companies – now what matters above all is intellectual capital. Manufacturing, logistics and the whole host of "hard business functions" can be outsourced to companies nearby or even overseas (although I always recommend keeping jobs "at home"). However, innovation can never be outsourced – it can only be sourced from within.

A good example of this can be found in IKEA's business model. It seems that every product in this penultimate Swedish company is manufactured overseas – such as in China – yet all of the ideas and designs are from Sweden, creations of designers who sit in the company's Småland and Skåne offices in southern Sweden. In this way, the company preserves its corporate character and Swedish design sense. At the same time, it is capable of competing in a highly globalized economy where price of manufacturing is key to success.

> *We have gone from an information economy, where information was power, to a world where information is a freely available commodity that is always just a click away. Ideas are the new power that drives economies, businesses and careers. Empires are made not of armies and weapons but of ideas. The road to the future is paved with ideas.*

Today, creativity is in high demand. The need for managers who are experts at employee relations, running assembly lines, reducing costs and maximizing efficiency has been eclipsed by the demand for those who demonstrate the ability to engage the power of ideas and to innovate. What separates a brilliant manager from an average manager is not their individual ability to work successfully on the tasks at hand, but rather their strengths in fostering creativity, in making new products, in transforming the business and in creating new ways of marketing, selling, producing, and engaging ever more diverse customers in a new, completely globalized economy.

The most successful "creatives" (the ad agency term for the "idea men" of yesterday) are no longer to be found at the advertising agencies or just at leading innovative technical firms. Creatives have multiplied and are found working in every facet and every aspect of the modern global economy. The digital revolution has transformed the workplace – and it has transformed what it means to be a worker and a creative. While "cheap labor" is still in large demand, the force of history is advancing us to the day where the creative abilities of people will not be suffocated by the mindless factories of the Third World economic necropolis. The end of the rainbow is within sight. Someday, and not many decades from now, I hope and expect that "cheap labor" will no longer be treated as assembly-line machines who toil in sweatshops and obscurity, but will be welcomed into new companies where they all may become the creators and designers of a shared future. Yes, I am an idealist, though also one who is eminently practical.

I recognize equally that for creatives too, the world has changed. Creatives no longer need to belong to a large multinational company to translate their ideas from paper to reality. Everything they need to attain success on a truly international scale is just a click away, so long as they know how to use the power that is literally at their fingertips (or more accurately, at their keyboard and a click away).

Just thirty years ago, would anyone have conceived of a world where one of the greatest inventions of all time, the Gutenberg Printing Press, would be eclipsed by the descendents of a counting machine? Printing made the publication of books on a mass scale possible. Mass education followed, to the benefit of all. Today, people read more than ever before in history. However, it is surprising that the world of printed books is heading toward mass extinction as e-books take over the marketplace. Most likely, only specialty printings, arts and picture books will survive this shift.

In this light, creativity should be recognized as the engine of revolutionary change, surpassing politics. These utopian, lofty terms are not out of place. Such ideas may be still reasonably challenged in nations where abusive labor practices mean that people are considered little more than "the best, cheapest machines." Changes are coming – often faster than you think. Concurrently, in the West, the companies of "the new economy," have realized that the currency of the future is the currency of ideas. We have a stark choice – we can either choose to become just another faceless worker and "one of the machines" or we can focus on creativity and leap into the future economy. In doing so, we too become agents of the idea-based revolution. Above all, increasingly, the choice is ours.

Despite this obvious choice, all too often, the focus of management is on streamlining existing processes and on just being *effective* in day-to-day tasks in the workplace. The work world is driven by targets, quotas and goals that must be met faster and cheaper than ever before. The time and incentives to encourage creativity are simply absent in the rush of business. This applies both to small retail shops and to the largest businesses where the paramount concerns are chasing quarterly targets, meeting sales goals, answering analyst expectations or addressing shareholder demands.

These business issues tend to crush creative thought.

Where creativity has no outlet, work environments degenerate and slide into inefficiency. Lacking incentives, the staff leave. They seek greater compensation and new challenges. For such stagnated businesses, the best and most motivated staff are the first to leave. Corporate loyalty is at an all time low, except in those companies where creativity is an openly stated first tier goal of management.

Like employee loyalty, customer loyalty is increasingly fickle too, following the "next big thing." As such, even the most high-flying companies stagnate unless creativity is invited, practiced and encouraged. These companies focus on fostering creativity *all the time* and not just at company "retreats."

> *As a professional creative, I am always astonished to find that despite the evidence that surrounds us of how creativity and creative processes bring results, only a few managers and companies are willing to take the leap and truly explore the power of ideas.*

Managers and shareholders are often confused by the rise and fall of their business fortunes. When they look at the basics of the balance sheet, products, services and organizations, they find few clues as to why they prosper or fail. More often than not, these companies are "creatively challenged." Weirdly, the same managers who fail to encourage creativity among their employees are often the very ones that will agree that creativity offers a window into a world of unlimited opportunity.

Thus, there is no better time than today, in good times or bad, to focus on the goal of fostering creativity in your company.

Ask yourself this – do you work in or run a creatively challenged company?

And what are YOU going to do about it?

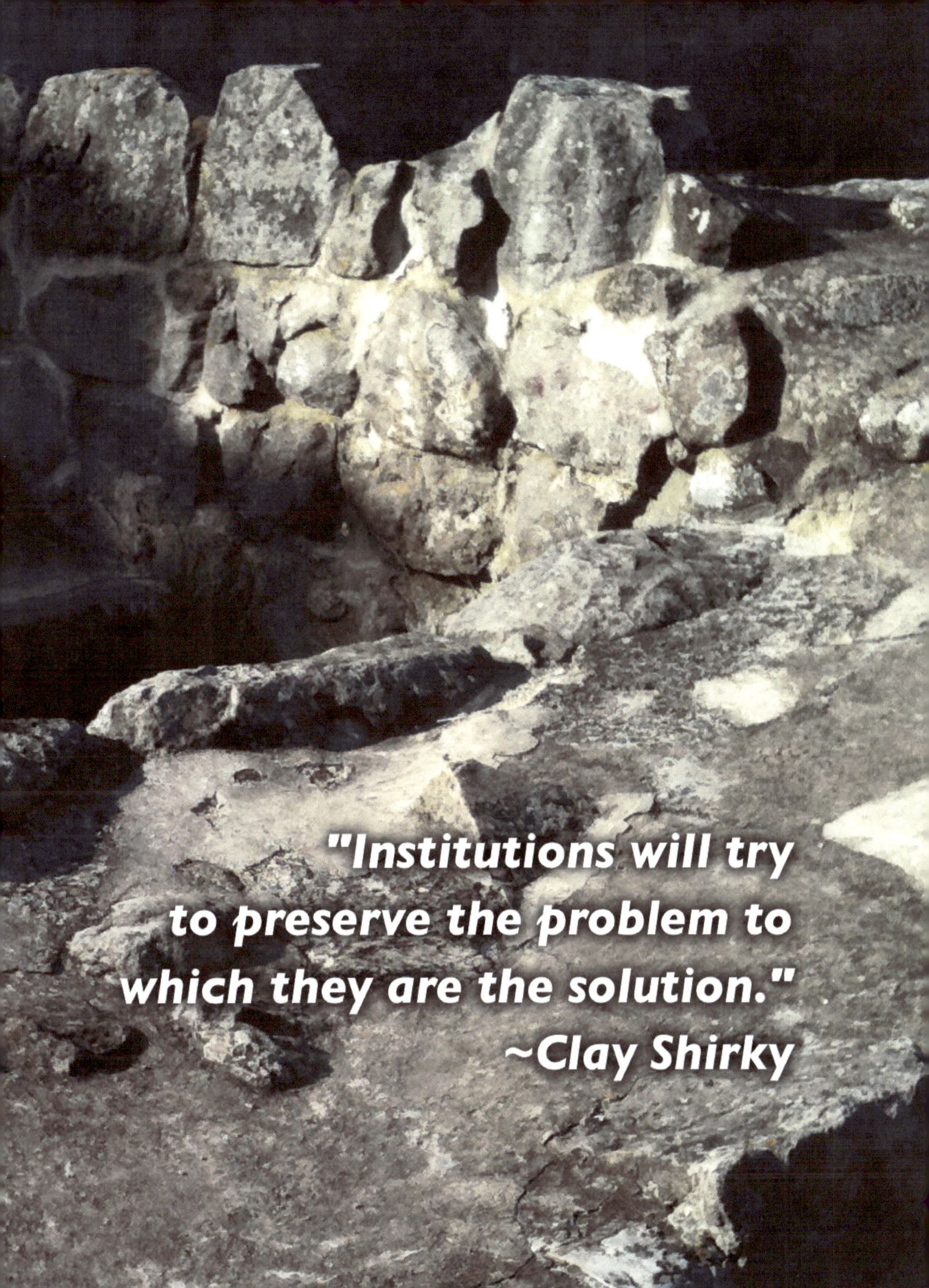

"Institutions will try
to preserve the problem to
which they are the solution."
~Clay Shirky

Chapter 3 – Creatively-Challenged Businesses

The very problems your business faces are your best guide to identifying your best opportunities.

The lack of a creative focus in a company can be discouraging, yet it also provides an incredible opportunity for a capable manager who steps up to the challenge. At a basic level, start by refocusing yourself to recognize that *problems equate to opportunities.* Even in businesses where creativity is at the core of an industry, such as in online media development and IT services, it is extremely rare for real creativity to be regularly practiced. This means that opportunity is laid bare for the creatively-focused managers are nearly infinite.

In creatively-challenged businesses, problems in the office are addressed with the knowledge one has, as quickly as possible, usually via a hierarchical paradigm. As an example, a catalog of products is developed simply on the basis of whether a product is successfully sold, and if so, on the blind hope that it will continue to be sold. Another example can be seen in businesses that are "one-trick ponies" with only one product or a few products and services that successfully sell. Once those products or services is identified, the management will "optimize" the business to pursue sales of those items, above all other things. Until the business dies.

In other words, at some point, as sure as the sun will rise on a specific day, whether that is a year from now or a decade from now, demand will dry up. Shockingly, the very same managers who avoided creative ideas all along the way will claim that they were not at fault for the demise of their business. Having avoided change, they will instead intone with grave seriousness about how they were simply "crushed by market" and that it was "unavoidable."

> *The experience of entrepreneurship is littered with the carcasses of failed businesses – many were once high-flying industry leaders that failed to innovate when the market shifted. Instead, a successful manager has to learn to kill their own business from time to time and start over within – it is either that or be killed by the ever-changing marketplace of ideas.*

Even the largest businesses and brands run grave risks when they fail to innovate. Consider these four failed companies and brands – all one-time industry leaders that are today merely footnotes in the history of commerce:

- Saab (the automotive entity, not the airplane business)
- Atari, Inc.
- Pan American World Airways
- Schwinn Bicycle Company

Each of these companies and brands died. Each might have been saved if management had approached their key challenges with creative focus. Yet these large scale corporate failures were warranted, despite being avoidable. Such failures are the inevitable result of mistakes by management. In each business, even where a history of creative focus was a corporate tradition, at some point creative business practices were abandoned. While each failed, often claiming to have been "crushed by the marketplace", somehow their competitors were able to succeed. Many of the winners in the competition of ideas were smaller companies with less potential, less financing and greater challenges.

In the end, and it may be harsh to write this, but the case can be made that *none of these companies were "crushed by the marketplace"* – rather, they were annihilated by their own management.

The Saab Story

First and foremost on the list is the famous Swedish automotive company, Saab. There are those who say that Saab could not be saved, that modern cars have just grown too complex for a company to succeed unless they have a critical mass and scale. Other say that Saab found itself in the wrong market, building cars for a competitive niche that was too challenging, what is known as the "entry-luxury" segment. Saab as an established brand never attained the scale and mass distribution required to succeed. Yet a closer look will reveal that its cars, in the 20 years that it lived under GM ownership, were increasingly undifferentiated from the mass of other cars on the market. The "entry-luxury" segment had moderate demand overall and, what demand was and is there went heavily toward more affordable cars with roughly the same performance and options.

Yet these same people who claimed that Saab was therefore "doomed to fail" nonetheless heralded the buyout offer by Koenigsegg and its backers, who desired to take over and return the company to profitability. Later, they also welcomed the acquisition bid by Spyker, a small Dutch specialty car manufacturer with its list of backers, including many from the former East Bloc. Both of these small manufacturers, Koenigsegg and Spyker focused on innovation and creativity in their business. Both did not suffer from a lack of mass distribution or economies of scale. For these specialty car manufacturers, the idea of shooting for sales of 100,000+ cars per year would be absurd – yet both were very profitable.

Those who looked to Koenigsegg and Spyker to save Saab held out that the creative aspects of those companies would somehow transform Saab to profitability. They were right in that hope. They pointed out to the profitability of Koenigsegg as being *in large part based on its narrow market niche with low demand.* In Koenigsegg's case, the market was for higher priced super cars. Strangely, these same people pointed to Saab and claimed its losses were *in large part based on its narrow market niche with low demand.* In Saab's case, the market was for entry-luxury, well-priced sedans.

This lays to rest the notion that the market wasn't big enough for the necessary innovation to stay competitive. What mattered more than anything was the management and its creative focus.

Similarly, one only has to watch the unfolding story of Tesla and the other new innovators in the emerging electric car industry to see that if a car company is struggling in the wrong segment of the market, maybe it is time to launch into a new area. Ultimately, one or more of these electric car companies will develop into the future industry giants – and Saab, like so many other failed companies, simply missed the opportunity to innovate. A brand can change – *all it takes is the right idea.*

Taken in this light, the story of Saab is shocking. This was a company whose very history is one of innovation and new ideas. This was a company with capable management, motivated employees and modern infrastructure. Further, this was a company nestled within the supportive nation of Sweden, which prides itself on being environmentally sound and innovative, with sound, fair and good workplace policies and laws. The company's workforce included some of the most productive, dedicated employees to be found anywhere.

Yet Saab's star still fell. Put simply, they failed to innovate and change. They continuously focused their energy on producing cars for the same market segment, despite losing an average of $5,000 per car sold. Incredibly, this practice of selling at a known loss continued for nearly a decade! If you are losing money on each sale, trust me, you won't make it up in volume.

Perhaps it is overly simplistic to state that Saab stopped innovating and died, but there is truth to that statement. Even for those who wish to blame GM for the stagnation that took place within the company, the fact remains that Saab was an independent entity under GM's ownership. Saab was alone in charge of its ultimate fate. GM would have liked nothing more than for Sweden's most quirky, innovative brand to actually innovate something and be successful! Somehow, however, that never happened, despite that the odds were actually stacked in its favor.

There are those who will claim that it is overly simplistic to say this, but like so many other bankrupt companies, the failure of Saab was avoidable. At the most basic level, the task of management should have been to refocus the company and move into new areas where its new ideas and innovations could bring new profits. To the extent that they did not do that, the company's future was put in jeopardy. Instead, the management viewed new ventures as unproven and risky – they were worried about gambling with the company's future. In retrospect, the caveat here being always that hindsight always enjoys 20-20 vision, Saab had nothing to lose – or perhaps it would be better to say that they had everything to lose. With the complete failure of the company, it seems obvious that such "gambles" would have been worth taking.

At the end, experts claimed that one of the contributing factors to the company's failure was the pressure of time. Saab had too little time to fix itself, they claimed, ignoring that the problem had been ten years in the making. Faced with nearly a decade to try something new, the company never did. Companies at this scale do not die overnight – it takes years for their star to fall. There is ample warning given all along the way. The opportunity to change course is there for the taking.

Certainly, these are simplifications, but they are instructive ones at that. They hold a grain of truth – even a loaf of truth. Obviously, a major turnaround in the auto industry is easier said than done. Yet the unavoidable truth remains that the company never changed its core business model. Instead, it stuck with a losing model right to the end. As a result, after a decade long slide into serious debt, it ended up in such a precarious position that it could not save itself. Ultimately, it could not even sell itself to a foreign owner. The weight of its problems and debts were simply crushing. Newly modernized factory facilities were shuttered and thousands of workers were let go. An entire province of Sweden suffered a localized economic meltdown as a result.

Anything would have been better than bankruptcy and liquidation. One wonders if some segment of the company could have broken away and started anew based on a new idea and direction. Some portion of the once great brand could have spun off from the failed giant perhaps. Perhaps an electric car division? That was the obvious option to everyone, yet it was not to be. In the end, the management at Saab was reduced to the task of seeking out a few tens of millions of dollars here and there in hopes of dragging out the inevitable date of its final bankruptcy. In the end, even that hope was reduced to just trying to find a buyer at the end.

The electric car company Tesla started with less money than Saab squandered monthly as it steadfastly pursued a demise, drowned in a tidal wave of debt.

Atari Turned Inward, Curled Up and Died

The sordid story of Atari is equally terrible. Atari was a start-up computer company with a graphically elegant, innovative product. Within the short span of a few years, the company came to dominate a major segment of the PC marketplace. Then, after a relatively short run, Atari seemingly ran out of ideas. Where other PC competitors brought out market-changing concepts like Open Architecture (which sealed IBM's leadership of the PC marketplace) and developed innovative programs to allow external software developers to build programs for their platforms, Atari instead focused inward.

The other PC companies engaged the power of ideas to advance themselves faster. They secured the necessary financing and develop the larger distribution networks. In the end, this allowed them to outcompete the manufacturer of one of the finest personal computers of its day. Atari had all but sewn up the games segment of the market – still a leading sector 15 years after the failure of Atari. Instead of adjusting, innovating and addressing the changes in the marketplace, Atari stood idly by. First Nintendo and then other game computing companies emerged with new designs, new interfaces and new paradigms of the gaming experience. The writing was on the wall, yet Atari did nothing to reverse its course and turn outward to the wide, global developer community for games and ideas.

In this light, the failure of Atari was inevitable. The demand for its key offering – high quality graphics for digital gaming – continued to grow. In fact, their key market segment flourished – yet Atari still failed and went bankrupt. Decades later, the reputation and quality of Atari is still remembered by fans worldwide. Many former Atari fans still have their old Ataris running at home, even today. A cottage industry of Atari programs has sprung up around the Internet. Some still hope that the once great brand will somehow return and reenter the market with a new offering.

This too is a feature of failed companies and brands. The very ones who were born of creativity and then, with maturity, choose to stop innovating may retain a loyal customer base even beyond their bankruptcy and death.

The lesson of Atari is two-fold: first, even the most innovative companies can stagnate and die; and second, innovation is a powerful force in building customer loyalty for the long term.

The Crash of Pan American World Airways

Likewise, the story of the rise and fall of Pan American World Airways is a story of innovation that turned to stagnation, decline and death – except that with Pan Am, the story played out on an incredibly large scale. Like Saab and Atari, Pan Am was the most innovative force in the entire airline industry. The company was the dominant American air carrier. Pan Am was arguably the most powerful, largest and greatest airline brand in the history of commercial aviation. Other great names of that era of US aviation history included Delta Airlines, American Airlines, United Airlines, among many others – while they survived, Pan Am did not. The question is why?

Throughout the period that its founder, Juan Trippe, ran the airline, Pan Am was the most innovative airline in the world. Many airline firsts can be chalked up to Pan Am, including some that are so commonplace today that it is hard to think of them as once being "new ideas." These things became the key differentiators for Pan Am on the way to it becoming the world's largest airline. Among these "early firsts" are the following (selected from a very long list) that gave Pan Am extraordinary market advantages at various stages of its development:

- First airline to use radios on its airplanes.
- First airline to use multiengine aircraft on regularly scheduled routes.
- First airline to carry emergency equipment on board for passenger safety.
- First airline to force manufacturers to build an aircraft to their design requirements.
- First airline to employ cabin crew (stewards and stewardesses).
- First airline to serve food and beverages in flight.
- First airline to use weather forecasting for route planning.
- And from the start – the first airline to operate non-seaplanes on overwater routes.

Those firsts are selected from the earliest decades of Pan Am's growth. The same level of innovation can be shown in every decade that followed until the 1980s. Then, quite suddenly and abruptly, the list of firsts ends. While other airlines continued to create new industry practices and pioneer new ways of doing business, Pan Am's firsts suddenly reads like a list of newly opened routes. In other words, as profits tanked, they were no longer innovating, but rather had shifted to applying their existing practices to more markets, over and over doing the same failed thing while hoping for different results.

Yes, that is the very definition of crazy.

It can be argued that the company made no major innovative changes at all after 1981, the very year that Juan Trippe passed away. In other words, with the death of Juan Trippe, his influence and his new ideas also disappeared from the airline's boardroom. On that very day, the end had begun.

Pan Am first came to risk *only after* Juan Trippe's retirement. With deregulation, competitive pressures hit all of the great airlines hard and in some ways unequally so. While some innovated and adjusted, others did not. In the worst cases, some airlines innovated in the wrong ways and became the first casualties in a changing industry. Yet to argue the deregulation killed Pan Am is false. The evidence is there for the taking – many of its contemporaries not only survived the era of deregulation, but even thrived.

At Pan Am, a new generation of management inherited the success story created by Juan Trippe. Somehow, they simply failed to stay focused on what made the airline great in the first place – its ability to innovate. Compounding one management failure on another, the new management faced increasing pressures from airline deregulation and changing marketplace demand. Too late, they proceeded with the acquisition of a domestic air carrier, National Airlines, to try to bolster their position in the market. National proved an ill-suited match for Pan Am's business model, however, and only worsened their problems.

While Pan Am's management tried to do something at least (unlike Saab's or Atari's), they did the wrong thing. By failing to adapt to the new marketplace, they wrote the writing on their own wall. Management seemed fixated on trying to preserve its past methods and systems, despite the huge overhead cost of multiple-layered organizational structures. This further degraded profitability, used up cash reserves and put the airline into deepening debt.

Finally, Pan Am entered Chapter 11 bankruptcy protection, giving hope to its shareholders that it might somehow reorganize and recover. Yet there too, management dropped the ball – nothing they penned was innovative. It seemed as if they were in love with their way of doing business, even if it meant that the company would ultimately fail. It seemed also that an air of unreality surrounded the airline; the view was almost as if it was "too big to fail." The untimely bombing of Pan 103 over Lockerbie was the last straw. After soldiering on for another few years, Pan Am ultimately shut down. It flew its last flight in 1991 and the company was liquidated in 1993.

The Pan Am name and logo were acquired by a railroad company, which still uses the Pan Am globe and medium blue livery on its rolling stock.

One can only wonder whether Juan Trippe would have saved the airline. Equally, one suspects that the answer is yes, he would have moved ahead with new ideas, creative solutions and a new focus. While some airlines failed, other airlines of that era adjusted and changed their business models in new and innovative ways. Names like United, American and Delta are still with us today, whereas the highest flying airline in the world, Pan Am, is nowadays just a fond memory in aviation history.

The Schwinn Bicycle Company Disaster

Equally profound is the example offered by the creatively-challenged business of the Schwinn Bicycle Company. Once the crown jewel of the entire cycling industry, the Chicago-based company was owned and managed by the extended Schwinn family. Like the previous examples, it too suffered greatly from a lack of innovation and creativity. Its missteps were largely the result of shareholder squabbles – essentially intra-family arguments played out large in the context of a global business. These squabbles lead to paralysis within the company even as the industry and marketplace around them began to change.

As incredible as it seems, the emergence of mountain bikes was ignored by Schwinn. Faced with unassailable evidence of a changing marketplace, the company stayed the course with the same formula for producing bicycles with old-style heavy frames meant for street usage. Incredibly, over the following four years, the family shareholders stood by and watched while revenues fell by almost 50 percent. As challenges grew and budgets diminished, the company attempted price cuts to attract back customers. Thus, fearing new ideas and new types of bicycles, they simply offered the same product at a lower price instead and hoped it would save them.

One can only imagine what might have transpired had Schwinn launched an entirely new line of mountain bikes, perhaps with a new technology or advancement that created some product differentiation. From their position as the dominant brand name, with the financing and distribution networks in place, they would have instantly reduced the competition to a field of followers. With better leadership, they would have taken over the entire mountain bike market segment.

Instead, as they stuck with the same product, the family took its bickering and internal discord from the board room into the public sphere. Reductions in cost were needed to try to attain success. This meant that changes in factory practices and employment relationships would have to be implemented. Such moves would involve cost cutting across the board. Thus, Schwinn entered into a predictable fight with its deeply unionized workforce. Predictably, the union won. With that loss, even their chosen strategy of offering the same products at lower costs was never tried. Instead, the company continued to suffer from a higher costs of production. Attempts to compete on price drained money which was needed to update its factories. Facing tighter and tigher financing, the transition from a factory that built heavy-framed bikes to a new assembly line that could produce the new light-framed designs was impossible. As the market ran away from them, Schwinn refocused its efforts on marketing its old-style bicycles, to even greater losses.

The victory of the union was ultimately not only the company's downfall but its own. Unable to compete, Schwinn closed its main factory in Chicago. In a flash, the entire Chicago factory workforce was out of work. The only thing left for the company to do was to become an importer of bicycles from China. These would be rebranded with the Schwinn name. The once All-American brand was reduced to a company hawking Chinese bicycles that were almost identical to its competitors' offerings.

This story could well serve as the perfect fodder for those who rail against union power – that would miss the point, however. Management had it within their grasp to innovate, change, adapt and expand. Instead, it chose stagnation, discord and endless debate while the empire fell. All that is missing from this story is the Roman experience of wild pigs rooting about the foundations of the shuttered factory.

Even at its last hour, Schwinn still had a final chance. If it could have innovated new features to add to its bikes, it might have survived. Yet here too it failed. Instead, when the company choose to try to compete on price, selling the same bikes as others, innovation was left to the company's new competitors. Predictably, sales fell further. Lacking the lean and streamlined organization of its main competitors – other bicycle importers – the company's prices remained non-competitive.

By 1992, the company finally failed. It became the target of a low cost acquisition. The brand would survive, but with new ownership. Like all fallen great companies, the shareholders of the Schwinn family would suddenly find themselves looking back and wondering what happened to their once great company. Their boardroom squabbles were no longer important, even if they had consumed the owners' time for over a decade of decline. Today, old-time Schwinn bicycles made in Chicago have a loyal following of collectors on the Internet.

The new owners of Schwinn have taken the old brand name and injected new energy into its future, adding fitness equipment and new types of bicycles to the product line. The brand's reputation was strong enough to have retained sufficient market share. This allowed it to bring renewed profitability. However, the dominant position once enjoyed by the company was gone – forever.

All of this happened within just a single decade. Once the management and ownership had lost its innovative focus, the company instead became just another casualty to the forces of market evolution. Schwinn had within itself the power and ability to retain its position as the leader of its industry. In fact, the company had everything going for it. It could have become a driving force of new ideas in bicycle design. It could have emerged as at the leading edge company driving the mountain bike revolution. Instead, the company selected the "safe" path of sticking to the same old models, marketing strategies and manufacturing methods of the past. This set up a failure that, above all, was rooted in its inability to encourage creativity and welcome new ideas.

Learning from these Four Failures

Each of these four stories share the same themes. There are *hundreds* of other large companies and *hundreds of thousands* of smaller companies that suffer from these same problems. A lack of creativity and innovation killed each of these companies, not questions of financing, market structure or competitive pressure. The lack of innovation had a greater impact on the company's survival than issues of employee relations, unions, bank financing, advantages of product lines or international competition. The overriding factor that dooms most businesses is simply a failure to innovate.

In retrospect, it seems simple – however, hindsight is 20/20. Innovation and creativity are hard work. Reading the tea leaves and predicting the future is not easy. Yet it is equally apparent that rereading last year's tea leaves is an obvious recipe for disaster.

From day-to-day business challenges to large scale innovation, the marketplace in today's global economy is faster moving and more competitive than ever. Opportunities are greater than ever before. The speed with which a product can move from the back of a napkin to full-fledged production is staggeringly fast. More money can be made faster than ever before in history. The crown jewels of former business models, such as streamlined manufacturing and industrial processes, have fallen victim to outsourcing. In the modern world, everything needed to launch a new product or service is just a click away.

Yet despite these factors, many point to a host of business challenges that they claim prevent them from achieving business success. They point to many reasons that forestall their efforts at innovation. In doing so, they ignore how the fastest growing, most powerful businesses in the world today have all achieved success by focusing on innovation despite their day-to-day business challenges.

The bottom line is simple – everywhere you look, businesses and people are buying and selling things. Money is being made or lost at every turn. There is no shortage of business out there. Conversely, there is always a shortage of creative thinking managers with the knowledge, ability and techniques to design and create the next generation of products and services.

It is of these things that fortunes are made.

You can't depend on your eyes when your imagination is out of focus.
~Mark Twain

Chapter 4 – False Creativity and Innovation Challenges

As a manager and creative, you have to watch for opportunities. By this, I don't mean business and market opportunities – those take care of themselves – but rather opportunities to apply creativity. Also, you must be aware that we are surrounded by false creativity. This term describes how products and services often derive simply from 10,000 companies throwing 20,000 things at the wall "to see what sticks." Technology advances in fits and starts; fortunes are made and lost, products launch and either win or fail. Overall, "seeing what sticks" as a business approach to this complex thicket of today's market is a poor excuse for creativity – and it tends to obscure the real potential of innovation that is ready for the taking by creatively-focused businesses.

> *True business transformation comes not from the Big Idea but from a thousand smaller, creative ideas that bring success consistently and continuously over time.*

More disturbing is the way that the media crowds around successful entrepreneurs as if they are the gods of business. Sometimes, these entrepreneurs may be the real deal, but more often, they are not. Often, they are just the ones who "got lucky". What lessons can be learned there? Is your business plan to "get lucky" and somehow succeed in spite of yourself?

The media compounds this problem by responding to public demand for the details of each winning entrepreneur's "unique secret to success." Whole magazines are devoted to the topic. Fast This, or Economy Whatever – yet this is misleading reporting in the raw. More often than not, the great success stories they trumpet are simply the results of a sad and wasteful numbers game. The businesses that are featured may be the "1 in 10,000", but not because they were particularly innovative.

In other words, studying their management techniques or learning from their business model is pointless. They are little more than the ones who guessed correctly, whose own idea stuck on the wall amidst 10,000 failed attempts. The singular key that brought them success and wealth seems elusive – which only guarantees that there is a market for the next edition of the magazine next month.

In a creatively-challenged economy, for the vast majority of businesses, it seems that success or failure are little more than a crap shoot. Everyone innovates "something" and then everyone holds their breath to see what sticks. When it works, the shareholders celebrate. When it fails, they lose everything.

At least they are innovating, even if only by sheer force of chance. They've gotten that part right – and they win or fail based on just having the best of the current round of Big Ideas in their quiver. This is what I call False Creativity. I would term it True Creativity if those who innovated these ideas went a step beyond and continued innovating all along the way, launching product after product, service after service, each of which were unique and innovative of their own right. That is the hallmark of True Creativity – they are not a 1 in 10,000 success story, which typically amounts to a "flash in the pan" success story, followed by a quiet "exit" by the investors who recoup their investment and take their profits before moving on to invest in the next "big thing", if they can guess at it correctly.

Steve Jobs took his company and its one idea *from nothing* to become a company that prides itself on filing thousands of new patents *every year*. In other words, Apple didn't end with its first product launch of a mail-order personal computer. Today, as a result of its unending creative focus, the company's revenues are larger than the GDP of most countries in Africa.

What's more, companies like Apple attract creative talent like huge magnets. Their successes are based on new ideas. Everyone recognizes that. The most innovative managers and visionaries want to be a part of that. The risk takers seek out places where they can take risks – and be rewarded. They know that their ideas will have traction in such companies.

At losing companies, where management fails to foster creativity and sticks with the old, they see the opposite effect – those applying for the "good jobs" are the least creative, least innovative management out there today. These are the "Dilberts" of the workforce. They are the ones who are attracted to stability, the status quo and stagnation. In such companies, they can pursue their greatest loves – generating useless reports, holding pointless meetings and making empty plans that will never be implemented. Once they are come to your company, trust me, they will stay around forever – unless you fire them, create an innovative environment and move on.

Quality Travels – It has Wings on its Feet

If you engage creativity in your business, if you authorize it and encourage it at every turn, your company will draw the best talent and retain it for years to come. Innovation, even more than success, draws talent. There are many expert managers, true visionaries, who would reject working for a huge company in favor of joining a small, innovative start-up. An innovation that fails can even attract the best and brightest – that is how powerful the magnet of creativity truly is.

> *The story of business transformation almost always starts with a story of creativity. As a manager at your company or as the owner, you have a stark choice – you can encourage and engage the creative process for the benefit of your business or you can watch it walk out the door.*

Even Apple nearly failed some years ago when it simply stopped innovating. It was only when its Creative in Chief, the late Steve Jobs, returned to the business that the company reversed its fortunes and became a soaring success. What few understand is that when Steve Jobs returned to the company, parachuting in at the 11th hour on the long march to bankruptcy, he didn't come alone. He brought a new vision that attracted many top managers and innovators to the company as well. It wasn't success that drew them – it was the opportunity to innovate, to be creative and to belong to a company where the future was viewed as revolutionary. Together, they saved Apple. Along the way, they also transformed the entire IT industry with the introduction of the iPhone and iPad, bringing the tablet computing revolution in its wake. Truly, one should never underestimate the power of creativity.

In fact, given the rise of tablet computing, one could say that the very company that helped created the desktop personal computer revolution is the same company that will ultimately kill the personal computer itself. Undoubtedly, that simple fact is the best example of what true creativity is really about. Another company in its place might have continued to hawk the PC to its last breath, speaking in profound terms of the heritage and history of the company – "we've always been a PC company and we always will be...."

On the other hand, there are those who look at Microsoft and believe that it is doomed. They see the marketplace transforming and they see that Microsoft's core products, software operating systems and office software like MS Word are at risk. They believe that the company will die a natural death – that the end is inevitable.

Their analysis fails to recognize that Microsoft retains at its very roots a creativity-focused management and leadership. Never underestimate the power of a few thousand top engineers given free rein to transform the company back to leadership status. I would point out that this applies particularly to one with the deepest pockets, a powerful brand name, distribution networks and the organizational strength to carry out new ventures at the largest scale. Again, never underestimate the power of creativity. Clearly, the future of Microsoft is not based on the Windows Operating System.

Success by Default is NOT a Valid Business Model

Remember this one fact – if you gather 100 below average people together to run a race, someone has to win, no matter how uninspiring the competition may be. As a manager or entrepreneur would you be satisfied if your mission was to avoid being one of the 99, hoping that one time you get it right just by chance?

Surprisingly, most businesses operate exactly that way. The costs from "simply driving forward in hopes that it will somehow work" are extraordinary. Clearly, this is not a good model for creativity, yet it seems we live in some sort of weird "try-everything" economy. The IT and technology industries are particularly prone to this approach to "creativity". It seems that what is technically possible becomes inevitable and, equally, each new "advance" is welcomed as the new "cool, creative idea."

Thus, developers have combined copy machines with faxes, phones and scanners – not because it makes sense or because it is a good business decision, but because it was technically achievable. We combine a computer into our refrigerator, calling it the "foundation of the revolutionary kitchen of the future." Yet is it really?

Technically, we can put a telephone into a toothbrush too – would it sell? The bottom line is that it might sell – and it probably would sell well if every other product on the market was even worse. This is success by default at its worst. It is what you have to learn to recognize and avoid – like the plague.

Brand Power Fosters False Creativity

The market is also entranced by brand, as if having the power of a big brand behind a product or service will somehow transform a product into something it is not. This is yet another type of false creativity, where the entrepreneur merges a non-innovative product or service with existing, well-established brand and calls it a *"Big Idea."* Examples that readily come to mind are – and these are all actual examples for the marketplace:

- Harley Davidson Perfume – presumably, this was a fragrance that either allowed you to smell like your motorcycle or inspired you to ride? It failed – but shouldn't that have been obvious?

- Coors Rocky Mountain Spring Water – a well-established beer company selling a really innovative product, like, uh, water? Where's the alcohol and taste in that? Another failure – the company donated some of its bottled water stock to Hurricane Andrew victims where, predictably, it failed yet again when the recipients, who had carried home cases of what they thought was beer, realized that they had just plain water!

- Google Print Ads – even a forward-looking , innovative company like Google can sometimes make a mistake; this was a completely backwards product metaphor that involved buying ad space through the digital means for placement in local printed newspapers. It too failed, of course.

- Colgate Kitchen Entrees – this is my personal favorite, a toothpaste brand name applied to packaged foods; this is strangely counterintuitive, sort of like a barbershop giving away Chewbacca dolls to attract business.

Clearly, one should never overestimate the power of a brand. It is an important lesson to learn that most branded companies invest considerable energy in preserving the identity and character of their brand name, staying focused on their key brand attributes. As a creative innovator, you too must focus on the key elements of your business. In other words, it is probably a safe bet to assume that nobody at Apple is recommending that the company go into the coal mining. Or it is?

Beware of the Hypnotic Effect of the Big Idea

Creativity needs to be practiced all the time to be successful. As an entrepreneur, you undoubtedly focus considerable energy on the creation of the Big Idea. Sadly, without continuing innovation in all aspects of your business, chances are that you will fail. No matter how innovative you think your Big Idea is, it will not stand the test of the marketplace, nor of technology, logistics, financing, distribution, manufacturing or a host of other business realities *unless you continue to innovate*.

A company is better off with 10,000 small ideas than just one Big One. With that said, it is also true that a company is far better off with Three Big Ideas *and* 20,000 smaller ones!

The road to success lies in how you create, exercise and build on creativity to transform your next venture into a massive success. As a true entrepreneur, your Big Idea is what gets you up in the morning and makes you excited about the coming day – and the dream of success drives you forward. Yet your energy and creative spirit must not end there, at the moment you create the Big Idea. You must continuously apply creativity to rest of the business. You must seek out the Next Big Idea with the same energy as you employed at the start. Apply creativity is applied to everything from logistics and distribution to human resources and the accounting department. Apply creativity to every aspect of your business as you execute, day after day, month after month, until you achieve success.

In fact, this is where creativity helps the most – it is the key to success, far beyond the Big Idea and the "Eureka Moment." You have to allow yourself the time and "luxury" of being creative, not just once a year, once month or once a week, but *every day*. You have to allow creativity to extend beyond the focus of the next Big Idea and have an impact right down *into the weeds*, where it threatens to transform every aspect of your business.

Your victory will not be achieved in one great battle; it will be won through ten thousand small successes.

Your Responsibility as a Creative Manager

Equally, the thousands of small ideas and innovations that are required to fight your way to success do not happen by chance. They are not everyone else's responsibility. As a manager, it is up to you to create the office environment where your team is inspired to create, to innovate and to achieve success. It is up to you to foster, channel, guide and manage creativity with every skill and all the energy you have. You have to treat creativity as the secret, super power that quietly resides within every employee – you have to not just find the keys to unlock the creative spark; you have to use them too, every day.

As a manager or entrepreneur, it is clear that creativity-focused business is the best model to achieve success. Creativity cuts across all disciplines of business, from the accounting department to the marketing team, from manufacturing to warehousing, from distribution to retail sales. Creativity is not measured just in the power of the Big Idea – rather, it is seen as the combined strength of a daily process that engages, encourages and utilizes creativity to transform the business and the Big Idea from just that – an idea – to a success story.

Above all, use the creative techniques in this book to refine your business idea _both_ _before_ you launch and _afterward_. Practice creativity every day and every week until you achieve success. The best ideas do not always win – the most creative businesses, however, are almost always profitable. Through fostering ideas and creativity, you will reduce costs, avoid missteps and identify new ways to win, new products to launch and new services to offer.

The Big Idea and its Risks

A final lesson here is that while positive in many respects, it might surprise you to consider that this exclusive focus on coming up with the _Big Idea_ does more damage to creativity and the energy of innovation than any other thing. Once the Big Idea is launched, it can easily become the beginning and ending of all creativity within a company. In other words, the Big Idea smothers everything and everyone else.

Further, the senior management may believe that the company's Big Idea has already "been done" – all that is left is to execute the business plan with cold efficiency, on budget and on time. The error in their ways can be traced as the direct causative factor on almost every business failure.

Compounding this problem is that companies that discourage creative ideas also inadvertently broadcast the ultimate statement to their employees – _that they and their ideas do not matter._ Technology and machines do not express the creative spark. They are not innovators. People matter and, within people, what matters most of all is their creative mind. Management must make this clear at every point. Just taking a simple decision to encourage creativity and deciding to go beyond the Big Idea can have a transformative effect on the business. However, bear in mind that this transformative effect will be temporary if there is no follow up. You have to translate policy and words into measurable action.

In this light, is it no surprise that most often a stagnate company's most creative thinkers quit and start their own ventures, often as direct competitors?

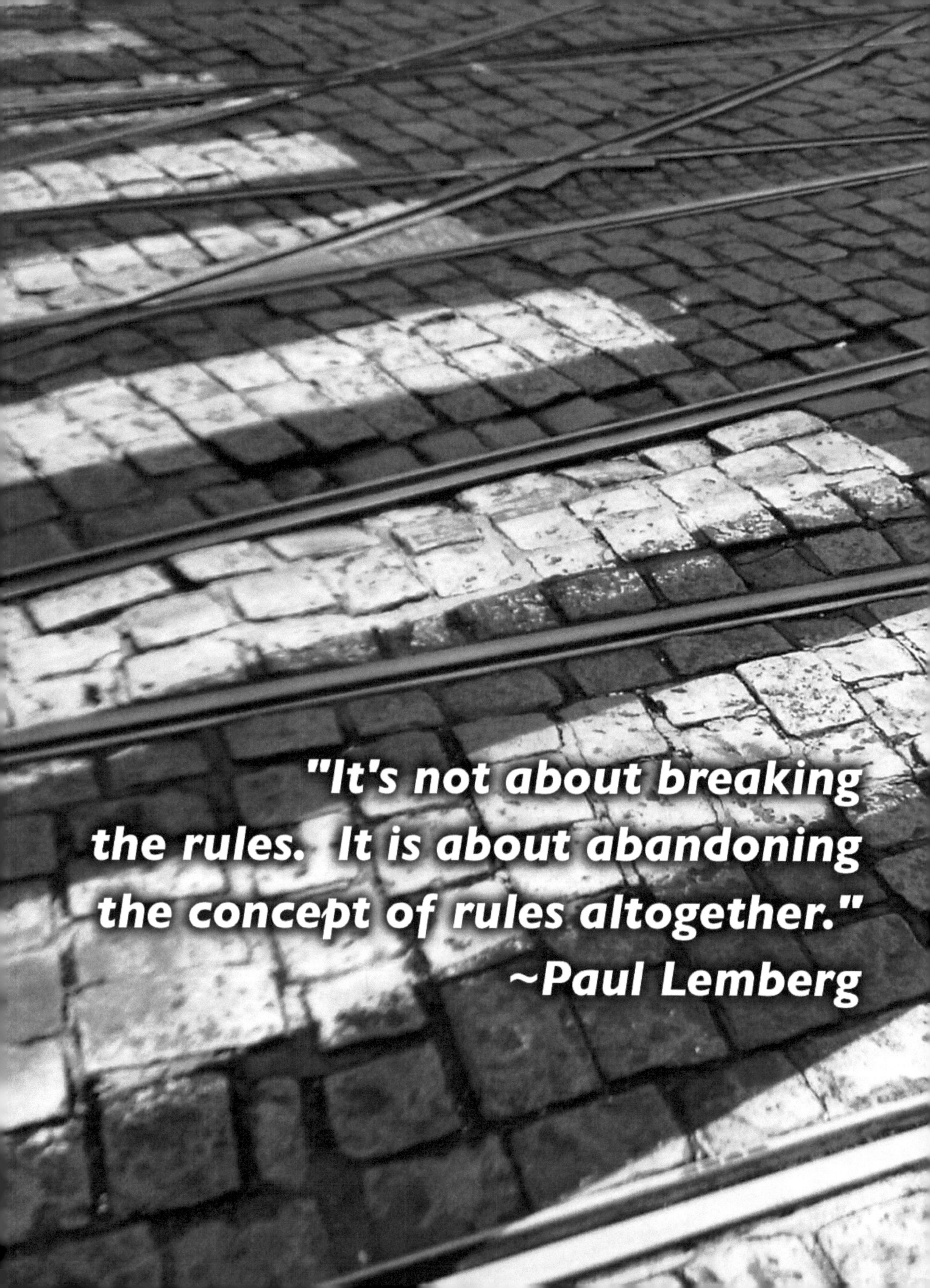

"It's not about breaking the rules. It is about abandoning the concept of rules altogether."
~Paul Lemberg

Chapter 5 – Questioning Rules and Using Creative Acceleration

Until this point in the book, much of what is written has been a guidebook highlighting *what not to do*. In this chapter, I begin the task of laying out the methods and means of creative thinking. From here on, you can read with confidence that I am firmly rooted in teaching lessons as *direct guides of what to do* with lesson plans of *how to do it*.

The stories of how creativity creates wealth and success in the start-up world are well-known:

- A college student has an idea and over months of late night work between classes creates the social media revolution called Facebook.

- Some tinkering guys with limited knowledge of electronics build a small computer and sell it as a kit for others to build; in so doing, they create the Apple personal computer revolution.

- A defense engineer working in testing microwave communications devices notices how a chocolate bar melts in his pocket and, instead of cursing, wonders if microwaves can make popcorn, and thereby invents the microwave oven.

- A small electric utility company struggling amidst many undifferentiated start-up electric utilities elects to give away lightbulbs for free to its customers; doing this, he increases demand, ultimately breaking out to become one of the leading suppliers of electricity – have you ever heard of Thomas Edison?

I offer a tangent here, though a reflective and helpful one – regarding the last tale about Thomas Edison, for 75 years from 1903 until 1978 – Detroit Edison gave away free lightbulbs. To the last day, that singular Big Idea was effective for the company's marketing. It would be effective today if it was still done.

So why did it end?

Incredibly, the practice was outlawed by a ruling of the US Supreme Court. The Court ruled the Detroit Edison's 75 year old tradition of giving away free lightbulbs was anticompetitive to stores seeking to sell lightbulbs. Thus, the curtain went down on one of the most successful creative marketing ideas of all time.

> *Never underestimate the power of an idea. And never underestimate the power of "the system" to kill your good idea, even if it might take years for "the system" to succeed. The time that takes is called opportunity – never squander it. Time matters.*

Taken together, these and many other stories are the focus of every entrepreneur and manager thinking of innovation. Let's go through what binds these stories together and how these types of ideas come about.

Applying Creativity in Established Businesses

Despite the obvious potential of creativity for building innovative, entrepreneurial ventures, surprisingly, it is not in new ventures that creativity has the greatest impact – in fact, creativity is an *even more powerful tool* for <u>established</u> businesses.

Why? There are three simple reasons:

1. Established businesses have financing or can more easily get financing to fund their new ventures and new ways of doing business.

2. Established businesses have existing staff and organizational depth to address the natural business challenges of employing new ideas.

3. Established businesses have existing networks and relationships through or with which new ventures may be launched and more rapidly penetrate the marketplace.

For these reasons and others, established businesses benefit the most from creative ideas and processes – yet all too often, creativity is discouraged or even outlawed. If you are in an established business that is doing well, seize the opportunity while it is afforded to you. Take the risk and innovate.

Do it now.

Creative Results Bring More Creative Results

An interesting aspect of creativity is that once a company sets out on the creative path, it finds that the results and benefits compound one another in accelerating ways. The first creative idea begets another. With each innovation too, more innovators emerge. When rewards are based not strictly on meeting targets but also on developing innovations and new ideas, the future of a company almost always shines brightly. I call this *Creative Acceleration.*

In the business of fighter aircraft, it is often said that stability is the enemy of maneuverability. A stable airplane is easy to fly and safer for the pilot. Sadly, it is also easier to shoot down. Obviously, getting shot down is not the safest thing for a fighter pilot. The corollary of this is that a highly maneuverable airplane is very difficult to fly. It is also the most deadly aircraft in the skies when pitted against its enemies. It requires the very best pilots. The best pilots, in turn, are attracted to the fastest, most unstable and maneuverable airplanes. The same is true in business.

For managers, the challenge is to let go of all of the established rules and ways of doing business and to be open to change. That means literally throwing the rules out the window and starting afresh each and every day. *The key here is avoid stability – become maneuverable in everything you do.* Obviously, some rules are important – and those should be kept, yet most rules are better questioned than accepted. If a rule can survive challenge, it is worth preserving – at least until the next time it is challenged

> *Entrepreneurs often talk about "thinking outside of the box". Visionaries view "the box" from afar as the place where their competitors go to die.*

The fact is, the more innovation you encourage, the more innovation you will inspire. The staff, on seeing management accepting their ideas and giving credit where credit is due, will become more loyal, more creative, and more dedicated. Staff turn over will decrease, company revenues will increase.

This type of creativity model is predictable, obvious and very compelling.

The concept of Creative Acceleration both follows and leads into one of my primary rules of business modeling: "The faster you go, the faster you go faster." This is the primary thing I look for when reviewing a business proposal – if you can achieve that sort of business model and describe it in your business planning, you will be guaranteed financing and success in the marketplace.

The only question is why so few managers are able to abandon the status quo and strike a new trail into the wilds of creative innovation.

"The things we fear most in organizations -- fluctuations, disturbances, imbalances -- are the primary sources of creativity."
~Margaret J. Wheatley

Chapter 6 – Opportunities and Impediments

Problems are the best guide of where and how to apply creativity in your business. Creativity opens a window into a world of unlimited opportunity.

Let's examine what that actually means.

First, in the midst of everyday things, by nature, human beings are *not* inherently creative. First and foremost, as a species, we are reactive. We react to changes. We react to stimuli. We react to news and new information. We react to the new sounds, smells and tastes. We react to threats. We survive that way.

In technical, modern IT terms, the human race could be said to be based on a single computer programming term: OnChange. When something happens, we react to it. Without change, we fail to act; we sit back and enjoy the fruits of stability that come with the status quo. Creativity only comes later, either upon reflection or in the face of raw terror and threat. Often, by then it is too late.

This reactive nature of people applies as much to us as people and it applies to our businesses. Businesses are nothing more than a magnifying glass of human frailties. Typically, it is only when a change occurs that a business, its managers and the staff react. Even in companies that consider themselves to be creative and idea-based, the vast majority of energy and resources are dedicated to *everything but creativity*.

Managers and the staff are so focused on business as it happens – after all, they are in the midst of the melée – that they rarely take the time to freely think ahead and create. To do that, they have to divorce themselves from the rush of events and leave behind their natural reactive tendencies. In the midst of business, we are paralyzed. Only once removed from minute-to-minute tasks of daily business, can we become creative. That is when we can plan and dream. To foster creativity, you must set aside time for the effort required. You have to take a break from the minute-to-minute tasks of daily business. This is why a creative session works so well.

Contravening Traits of Businesses

You may have heard the old adage that "to err is human, but it requires a *computer* to really screw things up." I believe that it is more apt to recognize that computers are an extension of business and business policies. Therefore, this old adage could be more effectively rephrased as "to err is human, but it requires a *business* to really screw things up."

Businesses are slower, less nimble, less agile and less smart than the individuals found within its offices. Nonetheless, businesses are born of individuals and their ideas. Businesses feed on their dreams and plans. Above all, businesses are the best (or worst) expression of the rule of *compromise by committee*.

Therefore, for business, the status quo is both the enemy of creativity and its best friend. It is the enemy because if the status quo is effective, efficient and profitable, most businesses will simply sit back and enjoy the profits and successes that accrue. Resting comfortably, managers will somehow become oblivious to the fact that somewhere, someone is working on something that will not only compete with them but that could actually threaten their very survival. In some businesses, the challenges and speed of developments are very fast. No time is left to address the new reality once the status quo has been abandoned. You are either changing the marketplace or reacting when the marketplace evolves. Invariably, if reacting, at some point the business will declare itself to have been "unexpectedly ambushed" by the marketplace.

Sadly, it is typically only "OnChange" when something new will be tried. Often this happens not out of foresight but rather out of the need to somehow survive horrific marketplace challenges. Fear and threat bring sudden bursts of energy. Obviously, this is not the most efficient way of "shaping the marketplace" or "managing the business".

For most businesses, when the status quo breaks down and critical threats emerge, what often saves them is the strength of their organization, people and policies. Somehow, in the final burst of energy, a new idea is born that allows the business to survive the new threat as it emerges – or not. At the moment that profits fall, when revenues tank, when competitive pressures mount and when financing dries up, only then does management wake up from self-induced passivity and slumber to fix the problem. In businesses that are overtaxed, only then does management take the time and apply the resources to address the problems at hand.

Do not wait to be ambushed – form a creative team to assess marketplace future risks, to develop new ideas and to consider, above all, what your competitors are likely working on. Put yourself in their shoes? Are they innovating? Are they stagnant? If you had their capabilities, what would you do? Ultimately, never sit back and wait for inevitable market-changing challenge and threat. Get ahead of the game – be active in the quest. Never stop. Never slow down.

Traditions and Assumptions

Many factors drive inaction. For instance, how often have you heard your uncle's most famous words of advice – "if it ain't broke, don't fix it"? Probably a lot. Your first challenge as a creative-focused manager is to ignore your uncle's advice. This widely held view is but one example of how businesses and managers fall into creative paralysis.

The fact is, your uncle had it wrong. If it ain't broke, take the time now to think about how it might break, or how it might change or how it might be superseded. In other words, the last thing you want to be is the company that makes the world's best fax machine.

When things are going well with whatever you've got, take the time to think how you might fix it, or change it, or innovate with it. Take advantage of the luxury of time that is afforded by a stable, profitable status quo. Businesses have plateaus. Use them. This gives you the time and resources to be creative – and to fix things when they aren't broken, so to speak.

The next lesson is not to treat problems as "bad things". Rather, get this into your head as the Chinese like to say – *problems are opportunities, crisis is opportunity*. Equally, foreseeing problems before they occur can be a valid source of creativity and opportunity. I mention this here because it is important – but there is more to come on this subject, so read on, my friend.

You have likely heard people say that you "don't need to reinvent the wheel." That's your uncle again –

and once again, he's wrong. The fact is, sometimes you *need* to reinvent the wheel, or at least you should try.

The propeller-driven airplane seemed good enough until the jet engine came along. Then the jet engine seemed good enough until the propeller was brought back into play and bolted onto the front end of the jet's revolving core. That innovation launched a new range of high bypass turbofans and turboprop power plants with extraordinary fuel efficiencies. Those engines have long since taken over the entire marketplace. The jet didn't *need to get reinvented*, but that didn't stop the creative-focused engineers at Pratt & Whitney and Rolls Royce (the jet manufacturer, not the luxury car brand) from reinventing it anyway.

Your greatest challenge may be retraining yourself to stop awaiting the OnChange moment and start engaging the BeforeChange creative process. Even for problems and issues that are already apparent, where few solutions present themselves, businesses seemingly go from day-to-day doing the same things out of tradition and institutional momentum. Paralysis sets in when changes happen slowly, rather than rapidly. Those involved seem to idly wait for the big shift in the marketplace, enjoying what profits they have today without the foresight to see that a good thing never lasts. They fail to notice the daily, incremental changes that result in a threat to the business. In other words, very often businesses may define a situation as bad but not "bad enough" to warrant investing time and resources into fixing the problems they face. Like the proverbial frog in slowly warming water, they stay still until they perish.

Therefore, your job is to apply creativity *to all aspects* of the work and *all challenges* before you. This ranges from recognizing the true nature of things, to creating processes, to developing innovative products and services and to finding new ways to do business. This applies whether a market is seemingly fixed or rapidly evolving. In today's increasingly globalized economy, creativity is more and more the key to success. Above all, remember that the rate of change accelerates with every passing year. As the economy globalizes, changes accelerate and come from unexpected quarters.

Nonetheless, the status quo and the various plateaus of profitability that your business may enjoy, are useful because they give you the luxury of the time to innovate before the inevitable happens and profits drop, revenues tank and your business goes out the window. Therefore, your first mission as a creative-focused manager is to take advantage of that luxury, if you are in it, and get to work.

Yet the vast majority of people, even business leaders, struggle with creativity. Instead of trying creative solutions, problems are addressed one by one based on established policy or tradition. Managers typically employ tried-and-true formulas that have evolved based on personal experience or corporate institutional memory. These are what we may categorize as "90 percent solutions." In other words, while they successfully address 90 percent of the challenges that take place in a normal business day, they fall short when dealing with the last 10 percent of problems facing the business. The last 10 percent of problems are usually the hardest ones, particularly intractable and difficult. They also compose the greatest threats to the future of a business.

Similarly, the 90 percent solutions don't apply when businesses enter into periods of revolutionary change. This happens when new technologies emerge that create a basic challenge to the way things are done. It is in these times that the very future of a business is at risk. Often an entire business sector finds itself at risk – your competitors too are suddenly "ambushed" from an unexpected quarter as new competitors emerge and new products bring the very raison d'etre of your product or service into question. This is when marketplace demand changes, where profitability is at risk and, ultimately, where the future of a business is in doubt.

And it is also where you stand to make the most if you approach the problem with creativity, energy and focus. Crisis, as the Chinese say, equals opportunity.

Exceptions to the Rule

Before crowning creativity as the cure-all panacea, bear in mind that in some sectors and circumstances, creativity can be the enemy. I know that this seems strange to write in a book that proffers an unbridled hope in the power of creativity, but it is something that must be written nonetheless. There are many fields where this can be the case. For instance, procedures in airlines and railroads are highly refined. Emergency checklists are developed in advance because when an actual emergency transpires, there is no time to be creative – thus, the checklist is used unerringly so as to maximize safety. With that said, one should consider that a checklist is actually a good example of pre-considered creativity brought forward in a simplified manner for use in a time-sensitive situation. Clearly, if a pilot experiments when facing an emergency, he will probably try something that those who wrote the POH have already considered and rejected – after all, they applied the "luxury of time" to create a set of procedures that worked.

Most probably, you aren't a pilot or a railroad engineer (or working in another such field where creativity is circumscribed by policy). If you are, you already know when to apply creativity and when to follow policy.

With that one caveat, I offer that for the rest, creativity is the key to success.

The way to get good ideas is to get lots of ideas, and throw

Chapter 7 – Ten Creative Techniques

The goal of this chapter is to provide you with the tools you need to break free and innovate, create and invent. To achieve this, I offer ten techniques that are designed to get you out of your safe zone and into your creative zone – and both you and your business will benefit.

Be warned, creativity brings unexpected experiences and results. It is not for the faint of heart. With every technique introduced, I ask you to step out of your safe zone. Sometimes, I will go a step further and ask you to do something that may even sound crazy. While I'm not asking you to dress in a chicken suit, the risks are just as daunting. Embarrassment is possible, even likely. Actually, I am asking you to put on the chicken suit. Really.

Above all, the singular goal of jumpstarting your creative abilities is all that matters – and if it requires you to go out at night and moo at the moon, the results will be worth it ten times over. The future of your business depends on you, so be prepared to abandon the rules, step out of your safe zone and consider new things.

Creativity is the hardest thing to find, engage and use. If everyone could do it, it would already have been done. Likewise, many businesses lack the ability, interest or focus to accept and encourage creativity. That only means that you have just that much more opportunity to innovate. Therefore, when you use creativity correctly, you will enjoy disproportionate, highly desirable results.

In other words, if your industry seems stuck in the mud, incapable of innovation and focused on the same daily grind, then that spells OPPORTUNITY – *and not just a little, actually a lot.*

With the right techniques, even those who think of themselves as not being very creative can become powerful engines of business transformation. Creativity will become seemingly effortless.

Most of all, creativity is fun. And embarrassing. But mostly fun.

Introducing the Creative Session

Most of the creative techniques in this book make use of a core concept, the creative session. A creative session is when you gather your staff or your core team together to focus on ideas. Like in Hollywood renditions of the advertising agencies of old, you will hold a free-wheeling, often crazy and usually highly productive meeting that has one goal – to develop new ideas. These sessions are no-holds-barred, free-for-alls that are stimulating and incredibly effective arenas for idea generation.

How to Hold a Creative Session

The steps to hold a creative session are simple and in some ways not at all different from calling the staff to a regular morning meeting. A creative session differs, however, in the approach you take within the meeting itself. Most meetings are top-down affairs where management informs the staff of decisions makes, checks project status or assigns responsibilities and tasks. The role of the staff in these types of meetings is reduced to one of asking questions, understanding guidance and then, afterward, getting to work on the job at hand.

In a creative session, that relationship is turned on its head. The role of the staff is to inform management, which then asks questions, understands the issues and then afterwards goes out and gets to work on the plan. Huh? That seems easy to read but hard to understand.

Okay, put a different way, the role of a staff meeting is to manage the staff and get on with day-to-day business. However, the role of a creative session is to turn the staff loose and to ignore day-to-day business in favor of seeking out new ideas that will ultimately transform the business.

To achieve the best results and undertake a successful creative session, a series of steps should be taken. These steps will guide the team toward the right goals, encourage them in free thinking and create incentives for innovation. Additionally, when holding your first creative session, you must take extra steps to brief the staff, channel their expectations and prime them to be receptive. For most of your employees, a creative session is going to be something they've never done. Ease them into it. Don't worry about failures. Don't judge. Accept criticism, but make sure your creative session doesn't devolve into a bitch session. There's a method here – follow it as a guide and you'll be alright.

> *The steps outlined in this book are a guide – feel free to use what works and to abandon what does not apply to your business or office.*

Before Starting Creative Sessions

Before you undertake your first creative session, you should ask yourself when was the last time your business had one. If the answer is never, then you're in a pretty typical position. If the answer was six months ago, then you're working in a creatively-challenged business. If the answer was last week, you probably don't need this book unless you are seeking new ways to foster creativity within your team or hoping to shake things up a bit. I hope I can deliver for you in the last group.

Don't be discouraged. Most likely, your team hasn't ever met for creative sessions. Instead, recognize the unique opportunity you have to really create changes. Just holding a first creative session is its own victory. You will be surprised at how much it will inspire your employees and change the picture of the day-to-day routine. The creative session will be the talk of the water cooler. The opportunity to hold your first creative session has been laid at your feet. It is there for the taking. You are a lucky manager, indeed, because all around you are many of the answers you seek, lying dormant and within easy reach. Nobody has done this before – you are looking at a green field opportunity.

You might be concerned and wondering how to do this. Creativity seems so difficult, so distant and often so challenging in and of itself. Yes, you often have new ideas, but how many of them get the mindshare, budget, resources and time to implement? How many of them ever get tested in the marketplace? These are self-limiting thoughts. Strike them from your thinking now and never let them return.

Now, you are ready to begin.

Creative Sessions – a Step-by-Step Guide

The following provides a guide for you to hold your office's FIRST creative session:

- Schedule a creative session on the office calendar for a week from today. Say nothing else, include no other information. Just write "Creative Session" on the calendar. The staff will see the calendar event and begin to discuss it – if not, ask one of your trusted insiders to point it out to the others.

- Just calendering a "Creative Session" has a positive effect. Your staff will start to discuss what a creative session is. This will generate greater interest and excitement, all key ingredients you need to achieve success. Some will begin to offer and refine ideas. The naysayers will have their say and will be sidelined – if you manage this correctly. The staff will undoubtedly think of advertising agencies and the Hollywood depiction of what it will look like. Don't disappoint them – tell them that *this is exactly what you have in mind*.

- You can also introduce the concept of the creative session in advance and with subtlety. This will encourage discussion among your staff and help break through the initial fear people often have when faced with something new. You need them to be free of prejudices. Further, they may need time to come to grips with the unexpected experiences that might come from a creative session.

- Wait a day or two before announcing that the topic will be revealed sometime over the next two days on the calendar. Again, you're managing the staff's expectations and opening them up to new ways of doing things. You need to focus the creative session on something, even if it is a general topic, like new ideas for the company's product line.

- A day later, amend the calendar event from "Creative Session" to something like, "Creative Session: New Product Ideas" – this will really give people something to talk about over lunch, further increasing excitement and interest. Even if you doubt they will talk about it, you will be surprised – they will talk about it, in fact, they will talk about it every day. Time will distill their ideas into something meaningful.

- Allow time for the naysayers to voice their opinions. A battle of expectations will be fought and played out long before the creative session begins. There are always some who will be mired in the role of naysayers. Recognize that that they are often the key to identifying opportunities for change where change is most needed. Above all, feel no threat from anything that is said.

- The day before the creative session, provide funds for donuts, cookies, croissants or other food and drinks that will surprise the staff – task one of the staff to go shopping and get it done; give them time and funds to do it right and be sure that low calorie, lactose-free, gluten-free options, etc., are included and that any special food needs and allergies are accounted for. Get more than you need, never less. Be generous in this way and the employees will be generous with their ideas.

- At the scheduled day and time, gather your team together in the conference room. If you have a small enough office, include everyone that works with you – include even your most junior staff, the college intern, and the mail clerk. Invite the receptionist and photocopying clerk (if you still have one in today's increasingly automated work world).

- Include the accountants, despite their well-earned reputation of being rather dry, dull and not very creative (trust me on this, you'll be surprised at what creativity lies dormant in those accounting heads).

- Once the team is gathered, welcome them to the creative session. Tell them that the meeting is important for the company and the company's future and that it will be a "Creative Session" – the first of many to come. Point out that most serious problems actually do have serious consequences. It does not help to sugar-coat realities. Tell them that the future of the company is their hands as much as in your own.

- Tell them that it is okay to eat and drink throughout the creative session and that it helps fuel their ideas. In some offices, this sort of statement is unnecessary, but in most staid, buttoned-down offices, this is important encouragement lest the food go untouched until after the meeting. If they're not eating, then it is usually clear that they feel somehow held back, restrained and unable to fully participate – this is important to recognize and combat early on.

- Tell them that in a "Creative Session", everyone is initially given equal standing but that this will change based on the power of their ideas. Tell them that everyone's thoughts and ideas will be weighed equally and that the entire group will weigh those thoughts and ideas together.

- Outline the challenge at hand in some detail. Then nod to them all and make a simple statement: "I am asking for your help."

- At this point, it often helps to offer an incentive – such as a coupon for an extravagant lunch for two at a nearby restaurant. Make it something that you can put on the table in front of the staff or hang up in the corner of the white board. If your budget is truly narrow, put a bar of chocolate at the end of the table as the reward.

- Choose one of the creative techniques that follow and invite the team to participate. Select carefully based on the goal of the session and the number of people you will involve.

- Then begin.

The following section offers Ten Creative Techniques that you can start to use *today* to help you and your business achieve success, greater profits and greater market share.

Technique #1: Positives Contract, Negatives React

This technique is an excellent "beginning" approach for offices that have never before experienced a creative session. The strength of this technique is that it reveals hidden aspects of problems that may have gone unnoticed – it also allows you to manage the process with minimal risk. It nearly always results with something interesting and thereby generates greater participation in other, future creative sessions.

Often the true nature of a problem facing a business is hidden. Real creativity must be applied not only to develop solutions but first to recognize the true nature of the problem at hand. This is where the creative principle of *Positives Contract, Negatives React* can work for you.

To explain this technique, be aware that people tend to identify the most obvious aspects of a problem quickly but rarely see the subtleties and small issues that have important effects. This is a "positive" or direct approach to the identification of problems. The end result of asking a straightforward question is a straightforward, but usually incomplete (and sometimes incorrect) answer. Additionally, the focus on the direct approaches tends to *contract* creative processes, limiting new ideas.

Conversely, when asked to identify the negatives or opposites of a problem, people can go on and on talking endlessly about the most minor features of problems. On the surface, these "negatives" or opposites are not very helpful when looking for a solution. Ideas must, by their very definition, pertain to the business at hand – not to the business that you are not involved in.

This is where the second half of this principle comes into play, called *Negatives React*. This term simply means that your reaction to the negatives of the problem may give you dramatic insights into aspects of problems that you may have missed. This can spawn new ideas.

The technique of *Positives Contract, Negatives React* requires a creative session. Further, it requires you to orchestrate a bit of managed surprise. Here are the steps to follow:

PHASE 1: Positives Attract

- Include everyone in the office in your creative session, even the most junior members. The creative session will involve not one, but *two meetings* – the first will involve the definition of the problems; the second will present ideas and creative solutions. Calendar the two parts of the creative session ahead of time.

- At the first session, inform the staff of the problem that is the focus of the meeting. Then, have the office form into small groups – perhaps just two groups, perhaps more if your office is particularly large. Make sure that no group has at least three and more than seven people in it. Each group should write a list of 20 things that describe the problem and its impact on the business.

- Give the groups five or ten minutes to do this – encourage them to discuss things amongst themselves. We call this stage, "Creating the List of Positives."

- Ask each team to present its list of 20 words/things. Write them on a white board as they talk.

- Once all of the teams have provided their lists, ask if there is anything to add – this may result in a lengthy session of people adding new words, which is quite welcome. Sometimes, the most awesome points are raised at this stage as the ideas of the various groups spur each other on to think of other things.

- Once this is accomplished, most will feel that all of the aspects of the problem will have been completely defined – they will soon learn that they are incorrect. Declare this stage of the process completed.

Despite the shortcomings of this first stage of the process, it still creates a generally valid and often deeper understanding of the problem at hand. At worst, it becomes a recap of what everyone already knows. In the worst case, this is still a useful step as a means of focusing people on the problem at hand.

The next phase of this first meeting in the creative exercise involves a process that sweeps away some of the misconceptions. It opens the door to new and creative thinking about the problem and potential solutions. We call this stage, "Negatives React," and this is accomplished with the following steps:

- Ask the participants to move and form new teams – mix them up. You need new bonds and new partners and groups in this step to get the best results.

- Ask the participants in the room to describe the problem, the challenge, company, product or service – whatever the topic it is that is before you – except that now, instead, they are to employ negative terms. They should describe, for instance, what it is NOT. This list you should call, "Creating the List of Negatives."

- Have them list all of the aspects they can think of that *do not apply to* or do not describe the problem at hand. Make them work at coming up with negatives, for instance, if faced with defining the true nature of the movie action hero, Chuck Norris, a series of negatives (or opposites) may include adjectives like: weak, indecisive, a nerd, etc.

- Make clear that nothing is too far out to be considered – encourage them to think without limits and to use humor (often helpful in identifying the true nature of issues). Make sure that they understand that there can be no embarrassment at this stage – we all have an opportunity to laugh at ourselves as we go along.

- When all of the groups have made their lists of all of the negatives, once again, they should present them. Write those terms on the board as well, alongside the List of Positives. As before, keep going until nothing is left to add.

- This completes the "definition phase."

The next steps are the most surprising ones:

- As a group, carefully examine the List of Negatives – for each and every one negative on the list, ask those in the room to offer an antonym. For instance, the antonym of "weak" would be "strong," the antonym of "indecisive" would be "decisive," the antonym of "nerdy" might be "popular," and so forth. This step allows you to broaden the perspectives and spot previously unseen characteristics of the problem before you all.

- As you go, compare this list of antonyms with the List of Positives. You will be surprised that some of the items differ between lists. Antonyms from the List of Negatives will include terms that were missing from the List of Positives. Any antonyms that are repetitive or do not apply may be erased.

- This allows you to generate a larger, more focused List of Positives – this is the only list you will need from this point forward.

The next phase of the creative exercise has to do with encouraging first generation ideas from the team. Based on the List of Positives, ideas may naturally begin to flow. However, you will likely need to spur the team forward with a controlled process, as follows:

- Ask the staff to form new groups again. This will create a different energy and further develop new ideas.

- Ask them to again review the original problem together, this time making reference to the new List of Positives so as to better recognize all of the attributes of the problem at hand.

- With reference to the List of Positives, ask them to consider what are we doing right, what are we doing wrong, what could we be doing differently. What products or services could we create that would address the problem or challenge at hand?

- Give them at least ten minutes in the session to map out any new ideas and solutions. Tell them that there are no bad ideas and that everything they suggest will be discussed and considered. Remind them that there is no embarrassment.

- Tell them that at the end of the ten minute period, each group will present any new ideas or solutions that they have developed.

- At the end of the ten minute period, have each group do a short presentation of any ideas they may have. Some groups will have no ideas, others may have two or three ideas.

- Write down the ideas without any judgment, even if they sound impractical. You might be surprised, but the tendency you will have as a manager will be to offer judgment outright, even as you write the ideas on the board – avoid this as it kills creativity. Also, you will likely surprise yourself when you discover you were wrong about something and that you were holding the company back from a "Big Idea" that was there all along for the taking – if you only allowed it!

- Now that all the ideas are presented, take time to discuss each. Have the groups themselves offer the critiques. Have them rank the ideas on the board, either by voting or by discussion and mutual agreement. Afterward, award the incentive gift to the one who had the winning idea, whether it was an entire team or just one individual – do not forget this!

- Have the office break up into new groups based on the number of new ideas that need further evaluation. Assign each group one idea.

- Based on the schedule for the second, follow-up creative session this will be discussed next – in three days typically. Tell the staff that each group will present the same idea in greater detail in a short, "mini-presentation" of no more than five minutes. Encourage them to do PowerPoint slides or whatever presentation strategy most clearly works for them.

- Be sure to give the groups time to meet over the next three days to discuss ideas and new directions. I would suggest that you ensure that each group is afforded the time for at least two sessions of two hours each so as to meet and discuss their ideas. They will also need adequate time to prepare their short presentation.

- Each person should know that, no matter how crazy or out of reach their ideas may be, it will be discussed without negativity or recourse – be sure that even the most "sacred cows" are not off limits.

- Tell them that the best idea and presentation will receive yet another reward.

After the three days, hold the second creative session meeting to hear the presentations and discuss the proposed solutions:

- Be sure to assign someone to get food and drinks for the meeting – and properly provide sufficient budget that they _can_ go overboard. Also, be sure that you select a second reward to give to the team that provides the best presentation and idea – for instance, a free lunch to the best group at a nice restaurant.

- At the appointed time, welcome the team to the second round of the creative session.

- With some flair, announce a new incentive reward for the team or individual with the best refined idea or proposal. As before, leave it on the table or tack it to the white board as a constant reminder of the rewards for creativity.

- If necessary, remind the team that the food and drinks are there to help fuel their creativity. They should eat and drink while they work.

- The format is as follows – each group presents their idea in no more than five minutes; and thereafter, no more than 15 minutes of discussion will follow. This will keep the group on a schedule.

- Don't ever "shoot an idea down" because it costs too much or is impractical. These sorts of negative thoughts are what can be called "secondary challenges" that can often be overcome in a second round of creative meetings. In other words, if implementing one group's idea might cost too much, that doesn't mean that idea has no merit, it just means that you might need to hold another creative session to address how to reduce the costs of implementing the idea!

- At the end of the meeting, take a vote or select the best solution that was offered – and be sure to reward them all for the work done.

At least one of the ideas created through this technique should be implemented if at all possible. If the ideas seem impractical, trust me, everyone involves already knows that. Instead, hold another set of creative sessions in order to find ways to make them practical. In other words, above all, you must use the ideas that you generate. A creative session that creates great ideas that lead nowhere is to be avoided at all costs – it kills the future creative ideas right then and there.

Sometimes, a creative session simply fails to generate any new ideas. When this happens, the staff may be discouraged. They will be the first to recognize that fact. You may need to intervene and remind them that the problem the business faces is very challenging. If there were easy answers, then you wouldn't have to go to such lengths to find a solution. Having said that, schedule another creative session to try again. Whatever happens, don't judge anyone for their efforts. Encourage them.

Note that this methodology can be applied not just to the identification of problems and issues, but also to the task of identifying the nature of a target market demographic or customer profile. It can be used to evaluate and better underestimate strengths and weakness of competitors. It can be used to examine issues, strengths and weakness of subcontractors and partners. It can be used to evaluate interoffice politics, new company policies, and the employee's views on everything from the company to their job satisfaction. It can be used to identify weaknesses in an existing product or service or in a competitor's offering, thus pointing the way toward possible competitive solutions and new directions to take with the company and its products and services.

Ultimately, in this type of creative session, expect the unexpected.

Technique #2: Employ *Backwards Thinking*

Reading the title of this technique, you might be wondering just what Backwards Thinking is. You've probably heard that when something is backwards, that means that they are "bass-ackwards" or just plain wrong. Obviously, that's not what I'm talking about. Backwards Thinking, when applied from a creative process standpoint, is about seeing the solution to a problem by seeing it "backwards," as in, "from the other side."

For example, consider a business that is struggling with a newly launched product that suffers from numerous issues requiring technical support. Customers are calling frequently with questions and difficulties. The product addresses a real need and thus, despite its known issues, it is still in high demand. Further, the marketing arm of the company is in overdrive and the product launch is well underway. The problems with the product's reliability were unforeseen and now they threaten the future of the business opportunity. Advertising placements are scheduled to go to publication. Demand is only projected to increase. The train is already running down the tracks.

In this example, it is clear that the overriding concerns of senior management would be: a) the customer service center is over burdened, resulting in long delays for customer service calls; and b) the business faces unexpected costs from the customer service center's problems addressing the increasing requirements from buyers. These problems will only worsen as more products are sold. The costs associated with the expanded customer service requirement are killing the product's profitability, despite its popularity.

The standard solutions are all obvious. The head of the company would task the engineering department to fix the problem as quickly as possible. However, such fixes take time – and the launch is preceding, as customer support costs rapidly mount. Even if a modification could be quickly developed, the cost of retrofitting the fix to those products already sold may be prohibitively expensive. Most companies would simply endure the financial stresses and forge ahead.

Does this sound like a typical business in Silicon Valley? It is a story that, in varying degrees, has repeated itself thousands of times in the software development industry.

Now, let's move onto more creative solutions using Backwards Thinking. This will give us a good example of the methodology involved in this creative technique.

The first step of *Backwards Thinking* is to put yourself into the shoes of the customer. Consider the situation – customers are buying the product, even if they know it has flaws. They are reading product reviews but, in this example given, they are still buying it. The need outweighs the problems they expect to endure – does this sound like half the software launches of the 1990s?

Being a first-mover in a new market has serious advantages. One of them is that customers are willing to accept a certain amount of product difficulties associated with using the new product. As long as customer support is sufficient, the customers will likely work through the problems until they are solved. The first conclusion reached through a Backwards Thinking analysis is that what matters is not the problem as much as the fact that customers are not willing to accept waiting 30 to 40 minutes on the phone waiting for customer service.

A creative idea that naturally flows from Backwards Thinking would be to explore if customers would be willing to pay an optional premium for faster customer support. In other words, they get "standard customer support" for free and they may choose to buy "professional customer support" for a small fee. These types of fees could be charged once at the point of sale or monthly on an ongoing basis.

This sort of idea creatively translates a cost line into a new revenue stream. The new support service could reduce costs at the customer service center and may even turn a profit. Enhanced customer support could be offered as an "added value" to the product itself, thus artfully redefining a negative into a positive attribute. The profits collected from the "professional customer support" option might enable the business to hire additional support personnel for the free service, thereby finding a balance that works for everyone involved.

This is but one example of how Backwards Thinking can be used to transform a problem into an opportunity – and this probably leaves you with the question as to how to use this technique in your business.

The example may seem obvious, but implementing it for your business probably is not.

Therefore, I offer the following steps to be employed so you can apply Backwards Thinking to your business challenges – this may be done individually, in small groups or in a large creative session:

- The first step is to stop looking at the problem directly – head on attacks rarely work, whether on the field of battle or in business.

- The second step is to map out all parts of the business equation. We call this creating a "business map." Carefully list all of the players and participants in the business model on a large sheet of paper or on the white board. This includes manufacturers, divisions within the company, customers (by type), financing, logistics, raw materials, suppliers, accounting, and management.

- The third step is to carefully consider the problem and challenge you face from the varying perspectives of each of the participants that appear on your "business map". Putting yourself in the shoes of each, close your eyes, and ask these questions, taking care to ask answer the questions from that perspective only:

  - What are my problems? It helps to focus on one problem at a time, but there are some cases where the interrelated nature of the challenges makes it impossible to separate them from one another.

  - What would I do to fix the problems myself if I could? Do this from every point and perspective on the business map.

  - What resources, staff and capabilities would I bring to solve the problem from each perspective? Would I be willing to use those resources, staff or funds to fix the problem?

  - How important is the problem to me, from this perspective and, based on that, what would I be willing to do to fix the problem? Each perspective on the business map will likely identify different potential sources of financing, creative talent, partners, or supporters that may assist in resolving the problem. You may find, for instance, that the problem you thought was yours alone is actually shared with another entity or business.

- If I fixed the problem, what would result? Would I face more problems? What would those problems be? This is particularly important in determining whether some players on the business map may not want a problem solved. Some may be benefiting from the status quo and unwilling to allow changes to take place.

- How long would it take for me to implement my solution? How many days, weeks, months or years? Be specific.

- What if I had unlimited resources to apply and could hire another company to fix the problem? What would I do then? How would I benefit?

- Overall, take the time to sequentially and completely assume the role of each player in the business, relationship or product/service cycle. This requires discipline. For many of the players on your business map, the answers will be obvious, not very important, and so forth – even that is important information, however. Value everything because from those sources you will find the germ of the idea that will work.

When you are complete with the exercise, having answered the questions from each perspective on the business map, you must then rank the level of interest of each player as well as the quality of the solutions they might pursue. Identify their issues, their strengths and their weaknesses. From that, develop a list of things that your business could implement and whether or not allies and partners can be called in to assist.

You may be inspired by what other businesses might do (e.g., this supplier would have done this based on the way they do business, but we've never tried that). You may be inspired by the weaknesses of others (e.g., our competitors have this problem that we have never considered; we could try this, which would really put them back). Likewise, you may find that one of the players on the business map does not have the problem and the germ of an idea is in the answer as to why they don't have the same difficulty.

Backwards Thinking can lead to very creative solutions to problems. Above all, the key to success is discipline and endurance. If a business map has 150 different players, it will take time and energy to carefully and legitimately consider the problem from all 150 different perspectives. With that said, if a business map has 150 different players, Backwards Thinking is probably the right technique to use. The more players on the business map, the more applicable Backwards Thinking will be in finding the solutions you need.

Technique #3: "And" vs. "But" Exercises

One of the largest impediments to creative thinking is just three letters long. These three letters form a word so destructive, so discouraging and so terrible that entire businesses have been known to suffer from paralysis, management failure and even bankruptcy. What word could that be? The answer is surprising – it is the word, "but".

Never underestimate the destructive effects of the word "but".

It seems to be common practice that whenever someone has a new idea, someone else will chime in to add their thoughts. Even if they are supportive, it seems to be commonplace that they begin their commentary with the word, "but". Once that three letter word makes its entrance, all creativity in the room comes to an abrupt halt.

Your job, naturally, should be to OUTLAW the word, "but".

The reasons this happens are simple – above all, the originator of the new idea hears the "but" as a rejection of their input. He or she senses a need to defend the idea. As a result, everyone engages in the usual give-and-take discussion on the criticism of the idea, not on the idea itself. Almost invariably, the first "but" kills the idea on the spot. Bear in mind that, "Yes, but..." actually means, "NO!"

Surprisingly, the person uttering the word "but" rarely dislikes the idea that they are killing. In fact, the opposite may be true; they may be looking to share the limelight and offer their own insight and support. Once they say the first "but" the idea that they most wish to support is placed under threat.

Overcoming the power of "but" is a serious challenge. It has to be accomplished on an individual basis. Many managers suffer under the spell of the great "but" and their offices suffer with them. Ideas are unknowingly squelched, people are quietly offended. Introverted staff members retreat into their shells, sometimes for days, sometimes forever.

The "And" vs. "But" creative technique directly addresses and eliminates the poisonous effect of the "but". It works by replacing the word "but" with another three letter word, the word "and", which fosters creativity without limitation.

Never, ever underestimate the power of "and".

To employ the "And" vs. "But" technique, take the following steps:

- Hold a creative session – this is where the team is told the challenge or problem and then given the opportunity to openly discuss possibilities, ideas and solutions.

- Make a simple rule – every sentence must begin with the word, "and".

- If anyone hears the word "but" they are under strict instructions to call it out by yelling, "BINGO!"

- On hearing the word "BINGO!" or the phrase, the offender has to apologize and try to rephrase their input to begin with an "and".

As unlikely as it sounds, this simple exercise almost always produces new ideas and new directions. People find it fun and, most importantly, the term, "and" implies acceptance of the idea presented and thus it builds confidence in idea generation and creativity on your team.

An example of a creative session using this technique would be as follows:

- The session leader starts, "We have to find a way to get financing for the next month's product launch. Brad, what would you do if you had no limits or restrictions – how would you get financing?"

- Brad will undoubtedly say something like, "Well, we could go to the bank, but we've already been rejected...."

- "BINGO!" someone will yell, "he said 'but'!!"

- Brad must now apologize and rephrase, "I'm sorry, there is no 'but'. Okay, we could go to the bank and...." He pauses, uncertain....

- You turn to the next person in the room – "Sarah, you take it – start with the word 'and'..."

- She will then have to try to add something to this ongoing discussion, which takes on the form of a kind of stream of consciousness – "...and we could make a presentation to the bank's senior manager instead of the loan agent."

- The session leader then nods to the next person around the table who takes it from there, "...and we could offer them something?"

- At first, the discussion will likely go through some predictable ideas, none of which will be likely that successful – if so, keep going.

- Sometimes, the very next person will simply spout off something truly unexpected and innovative that is worth exploring. If that happens, don't stop – let her keep talking until she's done and then, nod and congratulate her – then immediately ask the next person to keep going – "Linda, keep going – remember to start with an 'and' – what else should we do with Sarah's idea?"

As you go around the room, the quality of the ideas will seemingly magically improve with each "and" that is spoken. By the time the session is over, you will likely find an answer to your problem. And right then and there, you'll find yourself saying, "Yes, we could do that, but...." And with that you've got the last "but" in the room.

"BINGO!"

Throw your last "but" out the window and get started.

Technique #4: Throw in a Cow

I know what you're thinking. "Did he really just say, 'Throw in a Cow?' – You've got to be kidding me." I assure you, however, that I have not lost my mind. *In fact, I rather like my cow.* Put another way, the key to my creativity is that I am in touch with my inner cow.

To employ this creative technique, you have to leave your comfort zone behind – absolutely. The cow allows you to do this. It provides a metaphor for injecting creative spark into a particularly difficult problem. Therefore, before reading on, I'd like to ask you to lean back, turn your head up to the sky and let out your biggest, deepest, most shrill and loudest "MOOOOOOO!"

Do it now, you'll thank me later.

Well, maybe. Of course, you also have to deal with the chatter outside of your office door.... A few of my friends have gotten caught in traffic mooing at the nearby cars – no matter....

The key here is the *cow*. Then again, *maybe it isn't a cow for you* but rather something else unexpected that you can bring in from your personal experience. You have to decide what you will use as your own cow – if nothing comes to mind, go ahead and try using the cow.

This technique is extraordinarily powerful – it can be done alone, in small groups or in the context of a creative session. It can be used on its own or even in combination with another technique. The steps to employ this technique are as follows:

- Write down your problem in detail and divide it into its component parts. Define the three greatest challenges within the problem.

- Now, throw in a cow and take a moo at it. By "throw in a cow", what I actually mean is to imagine a cow in a field eating grass. Imagine the cow is faced with the same problem.

  ○ He chews and absorbs the warm sunlight on this fine spring day while considering the problem with the interest and perspective of his life as a cow.

  ○ Now ask yourself this simple question: What would the cow do? Probably this will not yield that many ideas – this is because that is the direct and obvious approach, so to speak, the frontal assault on the problem.

  ○ Moo-ve on and ask yourself what does a cow need? What are a cow's interests? How would the cow use this product or service? Would the cow combine the product or service with anything else on the farm? What role would the cow play in the production, marketing, sales or logistics of the product or service?

- These may seem to be odd questions at first – ask them and you will find that the process works. *If you look into the cow, the cow will look into you.* In short, the cow may be the most creative technique you learn from this book. Or maybe your cow is named Warren Buffet.

In any case, simplifying your viewpoint to the aspect of the common cow can often produce stellar results and some very innovative ideas. This is particularly true when you throw the cow during a creative session.

Know this too – when you introduce the cow, people will look at you like you've gone off the deep end. When you explain how the simple idea of a cow created this idea (discuss your idea and why it came from the cow), they will look upon the cow in a different light.

Even the most jaded and traditional companies will find the idea of the cow interesting, if not amusing. If introducing the cow to senior management, you may find among the other ideas presented, the only idea they will remember is your idea, even if they forget everything else said in the meeting. The cow has surprising power in many different ways.

One technique that sometimes works is to do the exercise with another person – have them act out the role of the cow. In this case, between moos, the cow can also speak English and, trying to be humorous, the cow's job is to comment on your problem from his sunlit pasture.

An example of how the cow can help is best illustrated by this true story from one of my advertising and design firm. We applied the cow to the problem of a banking client in need of a new tagline and logo for a product family of retirement securities. They had tried a wide range of solutions already in internal meetings and nothing they found sounded unique or all that interesting.

By applying the cow, we came to ask ourselves, "What use is a bank to a cow after all?" We realized that for a cow, the barn is about safety. For people going to a bank, the bank is about safety, a powerful parallel.

The cow changed the direction of the creative session and the efforts of everyone involved. New ideas were suddenly popping up, everything from using a cow for the product logo to discussions about the growth of grass on the pasture, that it takes time to grow grass, just like it takes time to invest and build a retirement fund.

The comments and creative process went something like this – shouldn't the primary color of the logo be green? Money is often considered to be green too. Money doesn't grow on trees. Really? Isn't it sort of like that when you invest into different types of retirement securities? Doesn't the money grow, slowly and steadily, like on a tree? What if money grew on trees? It does – apples, pears, peaches plums.... Walnuts. We're all nuts. Cows don't eat trees, let's get back to the task at hand.

Silence. Then the receptionist asked, Hey, do cows eat nuts?

Soon, the discussions went from barns and grasses to sunlit fields. Better times, enjoying the spring, the warm glow of sunlight. We've got to capture that feeling, someone said. What feeling? The feeling of the warmth of the sun, the softness of that on a nice cool spring day – welcoming, nice, comforting. Sort of like love, someone added.

Banks and love?

Families and pictures of kids are all typical bank advertising materials – good idea, too bad it has been done. Still, there's something there we might be able to use....

Then, the discussions went back to the subject of trees. Someone added that the thought of a tree made them think about their family tree and ancestry. Someone else added that maybe rather than ancestors, one should talk about the family part – as in the family tree.

Maybe the right logo would involve a tree with a tagline about families, someone said. Another added that a tree would bring up the thought of how to grow something majestic over time, like a tree that over the many years to come goes from sapling to old growth forest in all its gradeur. We decided that we should use a strong, tall tree as the symbol for the bank. Someone suggested partnering with an online genealogy service (actually a very good and interesting idea for a giveaway/incentive program).

Someone else offered that maybe an apple tree would be better. Someone else spoke of two trees and how the security and retirement program could be spoken of in terms of two trees standing side-by-side, their branches interwoven as if in love. Based on this example, you can see how the cow exercise can lead to new ideas and concepts.

Bear in mind that some people never discover their inner cow. If a cow doesn't work for you, try something else unexpected. Whether it is HAL (the computer from the moving *2001*), a Bedouin in the desert or a KGB agent from an old James Bond movie, it doesn't matter – just try it. The results may surprise you. Hmmm, how would a KGB agent deal with the bank?

Some managers are afraid of looking stupid or strange when they propose the cow exercise. If you are nervous, bear in mind that if the technique of "Throwing in a Cow" is discussed, even if it is ridiculed, once explained a *good team* will still give it try. If not, then the problem you have may actually be your staff, which should get you to thinking about new directions as well.

When you throw a cow into the mix, you will be surprised to find that almost always some new perspective on the problem emerges, new ideas follow and a solution can be found. Therefore, one more time, kick back, throw your head up and let out one more of your best – make it the loudest MOOOOO (if not the only one) ever voiced in your office!

Moo it now.

Technique #5: Free Association

This creative technique is easy to do and is based on a well-known concept. You've seen the TV shows about psychology where the patient free associates on ideas – yes? Admit it, you've always thought that it looked like fun. So why not try it? You will find that virtually everyone on your staff will also want to try it too.

This is a technique that requires the use of a creative session. Here are the steps to use Free Association to foster creativity and new ideas:

- In advance of the creative session, assign three of your best writers the task of each putting together a single paragraph describing the challenge or issue.

    ○ Make sure that they don't coordinate or compare notes.

    ○ Encourage them to be descriptive, use as many adjectives as possible. If you have a creatively challenged staff, ask them to write with the extra flourish of a Victorian author.

- The following morning, take the three descriptions into your creative session. Have them read aloud and while they are read, have someone write the key terms onto a white board at the front of the room.

- Now, instruct everyone that the session will use *Free Association* to develop new ideas.

- Before you proceed, recap the essential problem that you are trying to solve – this will help focus the session on finding valid solutions.

- To begin, call on the first person to your right – call out the first word written on the board and ask them, "What is the first word that comes to mind?"

- Whatever they say, turn to the next person around the table and ask them, "Ok, based on that, what is the first word that comes to your mind?" The next person has to say the word that is the first word/thing that comes to their mind based not on the word on the board, but on the word spoken by the previous person.

- Keep going around the table, pointing and nodding at each person to encourage them to say what comes to mind based on the last word said, as opposed to the next word on the board. Quite quickly, everyone will understand the methodology you are using. Quickly it will become fun. Then it will develop into something else – something truly useful. You have to try it to experience it.

- After you have had many people call out the words that came to them, maybe even going around the room twice, stop the process for a moment to offer additional instructions to the team.

- Explain that any time they have thoughts or ideas that come up based on the words spoken –

they should call out, "IDEA!" – and at that moment, the Free Association stops and the idea is quickly presented and written down.

- Even if it isn't someone's "turn," they can call out "IDEA!"

- Once the idea is captured, start again with the NEXT WORD from the white board, continuing around the room.

- If a word or Free Association pathway seems to be going into a dead end, after five or six iterations of words, CHANGE THE WORD. In other words, move on to the next word on the white board and call it out for the next person in line.

- Continue around the room in the Free Association exercise until every word on the white board has been exhausted. From time to time, remind them of the business challenge you are addressing. Sometimes, you need to go through the list of words on the board twice to find something useful.

- Once the exercise is completed, read again the three paragraphs that were used to start the exercise aloud to the creative session participants in the room. This will ground them again in the core problem at hand that needs to be addressed.

- Then, carefully and completely review the ideas that were offered and discuss each one.

A practical example is helpful. Imagine a Swiss watch company that specializes in producing mid-priced, utility wristwatches. Month after month, year after year, they have seen the marketplace for wristwatches declining as more and more people rely on their smart phones to check the time. Few would have predicted that the wristwatch industry would face its most dire threat from the cell phone industry, yet it has happened. And now the company's shareholders want solutions. Despite 150 years of profitability, the company is suddenly in grave jeopardy, its very survival is at stake.

As a result, the company's marketing department manager decides that not only is the company's future at risk, but indeed, so is his own job and the jobs of everyone around him. Layoffs will come eventually – maybe not this year, but at some point. The challenge of smart phones is overwhelming the business. The writing is on the wall. Simply producing a more accurate wristwatch will do nothing to stop mounting losses from engulfing the company and taking everyone down.

The marketing manager decides to try Free Association to address the challenge. He tasks his three best writers to draft their Victorian prose into short descriptions. For purposes of this example, we'll only discuss the hypothetical first writer's paragraph identifying the problem:

"It was a dark and stormy night," the writer begins as smiles break out around the room. "The candles flummoxed (what's "flummoxed"? someone yells out...) and the profits were seen scratched in the sands like mice looking for bits of cheese. Hardworking watchmakers worked late, ignoring the tiny noises made. Something eats away at them, disturbing their work, giving them worries and the deepest concerns. They look up from their workbenches, imagining a time to come when great machines will do their work, great machines to be envied, indeed feared! And they imagine a time beyond that, when something else emerges – a great clock, like the sun, that hovers in the skies above, giving everyone the time of day, day after day, and obliterating the need for wristwatches once and for all! Ah! Lo! Behold! The great clock is the iPhone! And it is not in the sky, it is in their pocket! Knowing no answers, they return to their work, worried about the future, knowing that if not their sons, certainly their grandsons would face the grave challenge of the great watch in the sky someday."

Truly, this story is bizarre, but it is nonetheless reflective of the nature of the problem at hand and it reflects the emotional aspects of the business. As a story, it is overly dramatic, but nonetheless useful for the purposes of a Free Association creative session. Even the most outrageous paragraphs can inspire creativity – sometimes, they help the most.

Based on the paragraph that was read aloud, these words might be written on the white board:

"Dark – Stormy – Flummoxed – Profits – Scratched – Mice – Cheese – Hardworking – Tiny Noises – Eats Away – Worries – Concerns – Workbenches – Great Machines – Great Clock – The Sun – The Sky – Pocket – Hovers – The Skies – Obliterating – Answers – Grandsons – Grave Challenge – Someday"

The manager in charge of the creative session explains the methodology to the group. Then, starting at the first person to the right, the process begins....

"Dark."
A pause, then the first person says, "Night."
The second person gets the nod, "Moon."
The third offers, "Sun."
"Clouds."
"Airplanes."

"IDEA!" Everyone stops.

"Do you remember those old World War II movies where the pilots were synchronizing their watches before the big raid?"

"Breitling," someone comments. "Airplanes as a marketing metaphor is already taken, even though maybe there is something there...." (Remember to never reject an idea – write it down and move on to the next word.)

Note that the Free Association that resulted from the word "dark" somehow ended up with the word "airplanes." The idea that resulted is a de facto dead end and thus the creative session leader takes the next word on the board and nods to the next person to continue.

"Stormy," the next one starts.
She quips, "Night."
Instantly, someone calls out – that's been said, what's the next thing you have?"
A moment of reflection, then she tries again, "Lightning."
"Thunder," says the next person.
"Weather."
"Waterproof."
One of the people suddenly screams, "IDEA!"

Everyone pauses and the person asks, "Hey, whatever happened to Timex's old campaign, 'Takes a licking and keeps on ticking?' We need to try something that is memorable and unique – a mass market draw that people can remember. You know, iPhones don't do well underwater."

The midlevel manager writes a note to himself, "a mass market draw that people can remember." He also writes, "study Timex's old ad campaigns for inspiration."

Then the creative lead starts with the next word... "Flummoxed."

And the process continues.

If you do this for 30 minutes, most of the time something unexpected will result. The list of ideas may even be surprisingly lengthy. The team will have a good time and it will be a great way to further enhance office morale – in fact, people will be talking about the experience for days.

In the end, even if it doesn't work for you, you have nothing to lose from trying Free Association. Everyone has always wanted to do it, even if secretly. Once they are invited to do so, you can expect a few fireworks, some good laughs, and probably some new ideas that can be developed.

Above all, bear in mind that solutions for particularly difficult problems often require non-traditional approaches.

Technique #6: Attack like a Viking

Perhaps one of the most interesting and bizarre creative sessions is to put yourself into a foreign role, taking on a different persona and attitude. Once you've assumed that persona, try addressing the problems and challenges you have from that perspective. Using multiple different personas can produce excellent results.

Notably, this is very different from Backwards Thinking, which is linked to a business map and, as such, is directly related to the problem and business at hand. It is also different from the "cow" because it is not based on passive observation – the cow says what she sees – but rather active engagement, preferably with an axe in hand. With *Attack like a Viking,* you assume a role and position that is completely unlike anything that exists on your business map. You are a Viking warlord and you have a solution to problems – one solution usually.... You may want to try other personalities beside Vikings to further mix up the creative pot.

The steps to undertake this creative exercise are straight forward and can be practiced alone or with a few others in a small group. It is not a technique that typically lends itself to large creative sessions.

- Isolate your problem into its key elements – jot down the key aspects of a problem that best define its core issues and effects. Be specific so as to create a simple view of the challenge – one that can be easily "attacked" by your Viking.

- Consider these key aspects carefully. Imagine yourself as a Viking from one thousand years ago, wearing your helmet, holding your sword, sailing the North Sea. Realize too that Vikings were not all warriors, some were traders, others farmers, and so forth. They lived differently, however, and in that there is inspiration.

- Consider how your new Viking persona might encounter and respond to your problem.

    ○ What are your new strengths and limitations? How do those differ from your own? How would you attack the problem with the tools and technologies of that era?

    ○ What could you do given your different world view as a Viking? What does the culture, unique personality and viewpoint of a Viking offer to help address the problem at hand? Would you sail beyond Iceland in hopes of finding the New World?

- Give yourself a full hour to do nothing but consider the Viking perspective. Go through each of the items on your list with care, ensuring that each one is carefully addressed, either with your sword or axe, or perhaps through trade?

This technique will help you identify ideas and possible alternatives and to better understand what limitations and strengths you have. It may lead you to question what you could change within yourself to better address the challenges before you. Taking on different perspectives often reveals unseen aspects of a problem or challenge.

Thus, if the Viking within you offers nothing, try the exercise again with another perspective, perhaps taking on the role of Thomas Jefferson or Abraham Lincoln. Choose a different time period or country.

Imagine how you might address the problem as a Ugandan dictator from the 1970s or as a pop music star, perhaps a fifth member of ABBA? Put yourself into the role of a world class computer hacker or become a spy like James Bond.

All of these perspectives, from the mundane to the outlandish, have the potential to teach you something about the problem and result in new, creative ideas. Prior acting lessons are not required to use this technique, clear your mind and give it a go.

Technique #7: Competitive Assessment

Closely related with Technique #6, where you "Attack like a Viking," this creativity technique involves putting yourself into your competitor's company to evaluate key aspects of your problem. This technique differs from business maps. It does not focus on how your competitor might see your problem and how they might solve it, but rather it focuses on how your competitor works and what they are doing in the first place – in other words, the competitive landscape is probably the source of the problem in the first place. This technique is designed to better assess what your competitors are doing and to recognize their weaknesses. Rather than self-improvement, the goal of this technique is often to prepare the attack, to identify the battlefield and to go after the competitors you have and take their market share.

In business, a form of economic warfare must take place between competitors. It helps to uncover weaknesses in their armor and strategies. Similarly, by understanding a competitor's business, problems and solutions, one often sees new opportunities that would be missed if a manager was to simply start each creative effort with the definition of an existing problem. In other words, sometimes when addressing a competitor's strategy, you recognize problems that they have, even if they don't apply to your business.

This can be useful from a competitive, aggressive standpoint, of course. Sometimes the best ideas come from evaluating problems you don't even have in the first place. For instance, by recognizing the underpinning weaknesses of a competitor's position, you might uncover the reasons why they act in certain ways. In turn, that might reveal ways you could partner, for instance, by offering them solutions to the problems they have, thus undercutting the rationale for their business strategy and competitive approach in the first place. Or it might give you a new business angle or business sector where you could torpedo their key suppliers as a means of undercutting their stability. Business is a cut-throat, harsh environment – sometimes you have to fight to survive.

By putting yourself into a *Competitive Assessment* mindset, you can sometimes reveal core flaws in a competitor's strategy. You may be able to use these flaws as the foundation of a revised business strategy, for instance, instead of resolving your own issues, you could create market circumstances that are difficult for your competitors to overcome.

Examining a competitor's issues will highlight an area that you had never considered. It may reveal a strategy that you have never considered using. It may give you ideas for entirely new products and services. It may be that the ideas cannot be implemented, perhaps because you lack the budget, but that doesn't mean that the ideas are useless. They might just work as threats that shape a customer's market strategies to your benefit. While you might know that you cannot do something, your competitor may not know that and may be forced to react accordingly, to spend money on R&D in the "wrong direction" or work to shore up a business relationship that wasn't in jeopardy in the first place, etc.

The steps to undertake this creative technique follow:

- Hold a creative session – begin by announcing that the session involves competitive assessment and that the goal is to find weaknesses in the competitor's business strategies and new ideas for your own business.

- On the white board at the front of the room, write a list of key competitors. For each, using input from the full group, outline the core problems and challenges that each competitor faces.

- Working together, define their strengths and weaknesses. What resources do they have?

- For each competitor, estimate their organization capabilities in terms of:
  - Financing
  - Sales
  - Marketing
  - Staff and management expertise
  - Shareholder issues
  - Past performance
  - Creativity
  - Intellectual property
  - Product or service pricing
  - Product or service capabilities (in comparison to your own)
  - Distribution and logistics
  - Supply issues
  - Demand issues
  - Location and centricity (are they spread out or in one office)
  - Other aspects that you might identify that have relevance.

- Put yourselves into each competitor's shoes. Imagine what it is like to be working in the competitor's company. What would they fear? What are their limitations and strengths? How do they self-limit their activities, such as by holding to a moral code ("we don't steal our competitor's ideas, etc."), or through being preoccupied with other issues? What are their priorities in their business? What are their staffing limitations and technical limitations? What is the extent to which they can and will compete? What would cause them to change their behavior in the marketplace?

- Once that is completed, ask the team to openly review each of your competitor's histories. How did they get to the point that they enjoy some position in the market place? What trials and tribulations did they suffer along the way? Did some of them face the same problems you are now facing? What did they do to overcome those problems? Did they hire outside consultants? If so, whom did they hire? What can you learn from what they did and how they grew?

- Finally, review the lists generated from these exercises and ask your staff to examine your own business, products and services. What can be applied to the ways you do business? What can be developed or created? Ask yourself if there is anything your company can offer your competitors to help them (making money while simultaneously changing a competitor into a partner)? Is there anything your company can develop based on the ideas inspired by the competitors' efforts? Are there any new products or services that could be considered based on what was discussed?

All of these are valid questions and could point to valid solutions. Competitive Assessment sessions often result in very harsh, and even cutthroat recommendations for action. Business is war. Remember that. Take your arrows in the forehead. Shoot your arrows to kill.

Along the way, you may find that some of your team, even one or two that you would least expect, have extremely hard and almost brutal insights into ways to combat the threat of your competitors. Above all, keep an open mind to the business strategies that your team presents.

Technique #8: Network on It

The key to this technique is to convene informal, one-on-one creative sessions with other business leaders and non-business friends from your network. Keep in mind that not all ideas are grown at your office. Just because it "wasn't born here," doesn't mean it won't be useful. This technique allows you to actively "farm" ideas from those outside of your business.

This technique is best done individually and not in a creative session with the full staff.

Here are the steps to take to employ the technique called, "Network on It":

- Go through your personal address book on your smart phone or computer. Choose ten individuals with whom you share a level of trust. Be careful not to choose anyone who is in your business sector or who might have connections to competitors.

- Select individuals who have a wide range of experiences that differ from your own experiences. Find those whose the core competencies are different from those in your company – for instance, choose your daughter's ballet teacher, the Boy Scout troop leader, your neighbor who runs a home-based accounting business, your cousin who is in the military, or a friend who works in city hall, among others. Be diverse and reach past the edge of your comfort in selecting individuals.

- For the next two weeks, choose one person per day and schedule a one hour phone call or lunch. Tell them that you need their outside input on a business challenge from their own unique viewpoint since they are not in your business sector at all. Tell them that you are seeking new ideas and need their help. Buy them lunch if that is what it takes.

- At the meeting, whether by phone or in person, spend no more than ten minutes "catching up" and building rapport. Then with some formality, announce that you'd like to ask for their help with the business problem and that you'd like to do it formally. This will ensure that the discussions don't wander across the landscape to no useful purpose.

- Tell them that the session is private and request that they too don't discuss it with anyone (this is important for competitive reasons). In some cases, you may have to sign them under confidentiality agreements.

- Undertake the discussion in three phases:

  ○ First, you will define the situation and the problem completely and with sufficient detail to convey what's happening and why. You will have to prepare this in advance and you will need to be focused, concise and direct.

  ○ Second, tell them what your company's strengths and resources are and what you've attempted in the past, as well as the results (even if unsuccessful).

  ○ Third, ask for their input and thoughts on ideas and possible solutions, no matter how far afield and unrelated the issue is to what they do in their lives.

- Carefully take notes in the third part of the talk – offering additional information as needed and ask asked. Be open to their ideas – and never use that deadly three letter word, "but...."

- Don't disregard anything they offer – simply write it down. The real work after the session. Since they are new to the issues, much of what they say may not apply to your business challenges, so it is important to not judge anything and instead keep on encouraging them to offer their insights and ideas. Keep asking until they are out of ideas. They will likely digress into story telling – some of those stories will contain grains of the the Big Idea that you need.

- Expect a call back later that day or the next day with an additional idea or two.

Do this for ten days in ten separate meetings with ten selected members of your network. Once these meetings are completed, it is time to move onto the next phase:

- Collect all of the notes together and rewrite the ideas onto individual slips of paper – this is important that it be done at the end as it will refresh your memory.

- Be complete, summarize each person's input as they gave it, highlighting only those ideas that have validity for the problem at hand.

- Take at least an hour and examine the problem in light of the ideas that you have gathered. Consider your company's strengths and weaknesses. Examine the market place and your product or service or the core aspects of the problem you discussed.

- Many of the offered solutions will be clearly weak or beyond reach – but even with those, do a full assessment and imagine that your company adopted that solution.

- For each idea/solution, write what would happen if the solution were to be adopted. Most importantly, review what the results would be in terms of changes that might result.

- Consider if any of the offered solutions might work and what amendments to the ideas might help make them more effective.

The technique of "Networking on It" can sometimes produce rather immediate results in terms of solutions to a business problem. As a creative technique, it can also lead you into unexpected directions and ideas that might be worth pursuing. The key strength of this technique is that it broadens your perspective on the problem, bringing in diverse experiences from others and from unrelated disciplines and fields.

By asking for help, you will almost always come away with at least one new idea. Maybe the idea you find will be your next Big Idea.

Technique #9: The Creative Circle

This creative technique is powerful because it achieves two things at once: first, it enhances the strength of your network; and second, it creates a team of creative-based co-mentors that can help at all stages of your career.

A *Creative Circle* is a monthly or bimonthly group of up to five people, rarely more, who meet formally to address their individual businesses challenges and to share experiences. Put simply, by setting up a Creative Circle, you can formalize and focus your networking into a powerful business tool with many advantages to everyone involved.

The strength of a Creative Circle is that it allows you to address not just one or two major problems you are facing in a single session, but rather addresses all aspects of your business, your requirements, your strengths and weaknesses, both on a business and on a personal level – *all the time.* A key element that affects the quality of your Creative Circle is the level of trust you have with its members.

Overall, this creative technique allows you to learn from others' experiences and to see how various solutions worked or didn't when they were engaged. It allows you to build your network of relationships and leverage your own network against challenges you face, and tap into the networks of other members in your Creative Circle. The result is a vastly expanded set of personal and managerial capabilities that can be brought to bear. This will give you reach to assets and advice that you would otherwise never have had.

A Creative Circle can be a source of ideas and innovative approaches to your difficulties at all levels – from managing the office (which may not be a topic that one would want to discuss with your staff openly in a creative session) to serving as a balancing force in helping to shape and improve your own proposed solutions.

To set up a Creative Circle, the following steps can be used:

- Invite five people from your network to join you in a Creative Circle – be sure you fully describe the Creative Circle and its purpose. Tell them to be prepared to talk through a problem they have at work. Be sure everyone brings along a pen and paper.

    - Be careful that those you call are *not in your business sector,* since the goal is to cross-pollinate with differing views and ideas.

    - Stay at your own experience level in business. A Creative Circle is not about mentoring juniors, but rather co-mentoring your equals and each other. This way, everyone can relate to the challenges and issues with some shared experiences.

- Set up a regular "long lunch meeting" of at least 90 minutes. Meet at least monthly to discuss *only* business matters and to exchange ideas. Set a regular, recurring meeting day, such as the first Tuesday of each month.

- You will find that at the beginning of each meeting, everyone will spend some time discussing family and personal issues – allow that, yet keep limits on it and then get focused on the purpose of the meeting.

- Institute a formal, timed process for the meeting. Each person is given five minutes to present a brief overview of their current issues and challenges. Use a timer – this keeps people on topic and lends an air of formality to the process. It also helps structure the meeting and prevents it from devolving into a series of personal work stories.

- After each five minute presentation, allow ten minutes for the members of the Creative Circle to offer comments and suggestions, ask questions and make points or insights about what they heard. Again, use a timer to keep everyone focused.

- Proceed around the table with five minute presentations and ten minute comments until everyone has had their turn.

When setting up a Creative Circle, be careful that you don't include too many members. If your Circle is too large, you won't have the time or strength to allow each person their five minute presentation and ten minute commentary period. A five member Creative Circle requires at least 90 minutes of time, given that there is usually about ten minutes of informality at the beginning and ending of each session. Going more than 90 minutes in a Creative Circle doesn't work that well either as mental exhaustion sets in. There is a law of decreasing returns at work here – be aware of it.

Creative Circles can be life changing. Through formalizing your networking, you will be able to tap into a range of support, help others, and transform your business, your management style and your career.

Technique #10: Two Generations Ahead

This creative technique involves considerable intellectual prowess. It is challenging, difficult and takes serious concentration. The concept is simple even if the process of carrying it out is extremely challenging. This technique is best undertaken by the manager alone or with just one or two people. This technique is generally ineffective in a large creative session.

The following steps are recommended for best results:

- Engage your imagination by envisioning how your business sector will change in the coming months and years. Envision how the future will look once all the current developments have been completed and widely adopted in the marketplace. This step is called, "One Generation Ahead." To accomplish this, proceed as follows:

  - Carefully map out the status of your industry. What is happening? What are the products and services available? What business models are in use? What marketing campaigns are in play? Who are the dominant players? Who are the up and coming players? Who are the fallen giants? Which companies are in trouble and why? Which companies are successful and why? Which are the rising stars? Which have hit the peak and are at a plateau? What would it take for them to break through the ceiling that prevents further expansion?

  - Consider the impediments to progress as well as upcoming market developments. What holds your company and others back? Where are you heading as an industry? What new products and services are on the horizon? What developments are in the pipeline? What is the timetable for each new development? Are the changes technological? Are the changes related into international economics and international relations? Are there political aspects to consider, such as who is in the White House or which foreign leaders or parties are involved? Are there local political or economic considerations? Are there weather issues, environmental issues or zoning/developmental issues that are on the horizon?

  - Do not limit yourself to the obvious changes – include also the most daring changes and developments you can find. Include technologies or practices that are in the very earliest stages of development. Know your own directions; estimate your competitors; and include everything on a "Future Map".

- Set up a timeline, this is the a "Future Map" mentioned above, so as to best assess and record what the future will look like in a structured way:

  - Your Future Map should include a clear projection of when each of the changes you foresee will likely impact the market place and your business. You will find that all of the changes you envision won't happen at once – some are a year away while others may require a decade or more to come to maturity.

  - Envision your business at various points along the timeline. Consider how things will look one year ahead, then five years and then ten years from now. Imagine what issues you might face at that time. How will your company adapt? What solutions will you try? What products and services will be effective? How will this change your business? How will this change your staffing, your organization, your costs, your revenues, and your profits? Carefully assess and write down what the future may look like – document this carefully on the Future Map.

- Once this is completed, it is time to make the leap and go "Two Generations Ahead." This is thinking across multiple generations of future development, and is accomplished as follows:

  - Imagine that the Future Map is the new and concise world of your business sector in which you already live – imagine that all of those changes you have mapped out have taken place, for good and for bad, at the various points along the way.

  - Consider how the changes that come will create new issues (and new opportunities). For instance, are there new issues of resource scarcity? Are there changes in business structures and ways of doing business that will create new requirements? Your company launched this product – what product the competitors launch and now how must you respond?

  - What additional developments and new inventions will be needed to address the changes that are coming? Are there new opportunities that emerge based on changes that are coming farther out on the timeline? Your goal in this phase is to "invent the inventions needed to address the problems of the future."

- Assess what your capabilities are to address the problems that you can foresee through your Future Map.

  - Examine your current business. What are your strengths and weaknesses today and in the future? What can you do to start developing solutions now for problems that are yet in the future?

  - Ask yourself which of those opportunities could you start building today? What resources do you have to address these future issues?

This is a systematic approach to building not just the next generation's ideas, but rather two generations ahead. Done correctly, it can put you years ahead of the competition. The Future Map allows you to see the changes coming and start innovating today to address the opportunities that are yet to come. This makes it a very powerful tool for business transformation and idea generation.

A well-crafted Future Map can lead to far-reaching business strategies that create long term impacts. The Future Map offers the opportunity to start working now on the problems of tomorrow, yet with the luxury of time. It gives you advance notice of what you will need to put in place within your business organization, mission, products and services, staff and financing.

It may require *all* of your skills and creative techniques to accomplish an accurate Future Map. Do not hesitate to employ the other nine techniques in this book when developing your Future Map. You will need every ounce of intellectual strength, significant outside input, varying perspectives and maybe more than a cow or two to finish the job.

"Creativity is contagious, pass it on."
~Albert Einstein

Chapter 8 – From Conclusion to New Beginning

In this book, I have discussed the power of ideas and the importance of creating a business tradition that encourages and even actively farms creativity from your team. I have offered a set of ten creative techniques that can serve to help you achieve extraordinary results. Some, most or all will apply to your business. A few of these techniques might apply to one type of challenge, but not to another. Others may apply today but not next week, next month or next year.

The key to creativity is as much technique-based as it is to stay fresh and explore alternatives and options from differing perspectives. Continuously running the same creative techniques and sessions on the same topics will rarely yield different results. Conversely, some topics and issues may be so challenging that solutions are still out of reach despite several attempts to develop new approaches and using several techniques. These topics will need to be dissected down to reasonable components and addressed individually, since the overall problem is simply too complex for a single creative session.

The key to success is to tap into the creative aspects of yourself and your team. Creativity knows no limits. Those who provide creative insights may be within or outside of your industry. Some of the most creative people in your office may be the most junior ones.

Throughout the process, be open-minded. Keep clear of self-criticism. Accept creative alternatives from everyone. Be ready to abandon your comfortable and safe zone. Be willing to try new experiences and accept different viewpoints. Bear in mind that nobody has all the answers. Involving others is critical to the creative process.

The best way to get started with creativity is to just begin. Even if your office is reticent and others may discourage you, the time and place for creativity is now. Above all, have fun. It is only through fun and positive experiences that creativity blooms.

Now go out and give the moon one last *MOOOOOOO!* – and get started!

About the Author

Thomas Van Hare's career includes work in defense and foreign policy as a White House appointee. Over the last decade, he served on the Executive Committee to the Secretary of Defense and was involved in the reconstruction and stabilization efforts in Afghanistan and Iraq. He has served as president and CEO of an international airline. Previously he owned and directed a marketing and design firm with clients ranging from IBM and Goldman Sachs to KPMG, Martinair, Ingram Micro, Kodak, the US Army and others. He is a highly experienced speaker who has addressed major conferences and international forums on the topics of advertising and design as well as security and international business.

He is a commercial pilot with extensive experience flying search and rescue missions both as a command pilot and mission director. In that role, he helped to save the lives of thousands of Cuban refugees. He has directed disaster relief missions in over twenty nations.

A graduate of Michigan State University's prestigious James Madison program, he holds a degree in International Relations. He has studied for his Masters Degree in Global Studies at Lund University in Sweden. He has written other books, available both in print and as e-books, including the top-selling work with co-author Matt Lawrence, _BETRAYAL: Clinton, Castro & the Cuban Five_ and its Spanish-language edition, _TRAICIÓN: Clinton, Castro y Los Cinco Cubanos._

About the Editor

Helena Nolke is a writer/editor in Sweden who specializes in the business, marketing, communications, education and special needs. She holds a degree in journalism and has completed advanced studies in education at Florida Atlantic University. She is fluent in both English and Swedish.

References

Cohen, Scott (1987), _Zap: The Rise and Fall of Atari_, Mcgraw-Hill, ISBN: 0070115435

Crown, Judith and Coleman, Glenn (1996), _No Hands: The Rise and Fall of the Schwinn Bicycle Company, an American Institution_, Henry Holt & Co, ISBN: 0805035532

Daley, Robert (1980), _An American Saga: Juan Trippe and his Pan Am Empire_, Random House, ISBN: 039450223X

Dymock, Eric (1997), _Saab: Half a Century of Achievement, 1947-1977_, Haynes Publications, ISBN: 0854299815

Editors of Fortune Magazine (2011), _All About Steve: The Story of Steve Jobs and Apple from the Pages of Fortune_, Publ. by Fortune, ASIN: B005CRQ29E

Gandt, Robert (1995), _Skygods: The Fall of Pan Am_, William Morrow & Co, ISBN: 0688046150

Harris, Don (2011), _Pan Am: A History of the Airline that Define An Age_, Golgotha Press, ASIN: B0056BBYYY

Kamprad, Ingvar and Torekull, Bertil (1999), _Leading By Design: The Ikea Story_, Collins, ISBN: 0066620384

Kewin, Thomas (2005), _The Pan Am Journey_, Xlibris, ISBN: 1413486029

Lashinsky, Adam (2012), _Inside Apple_, Publ. by John Murray, ASIN: B006ZZQHME

Metro, _"Saabs konkurs beviljad"_ (Swedish), Metro.se, Dec. 19, 2011

Pridmore, Jay (2001), _Schwinn Bicycles_, MBI, ISBN: 0760312982

SAAB Automobile AB (2001), _Made in Trollhattan_, Lowe Forever, Stockholm, Sweden, ISBN: 916310704X

Saab Museum (2012), "Saab Innovations", www.saabmuseum.com/innovations

SaabsUnited.com (2012), _"The last Saabs have been built… *updated!"_, Feb. 22, 2012